AUTHORITATIVE GUIDE TO

Auctions

THE Blood-Horse

AUTHORITATIVE GUIDE TO

Auctions

**BY THE STAFF AND CORRESPONDENTS
OF BLOOD-HORSE PUBLICATIONS**

Lexington, Kentucky

ECLIPSE
PRESS

Library of Congress Control Number: 2003114576

ISBN 1-58150-109-9

Printed in the Hong Kong
First Edition: June 2004

Distributed to the trade by
National Book Network
4720-A Boston Way, Lanham, MD 20706
1.800.462.6420

A Division of
Blood-Horse Publications
Publishers Since 1916

ECLIPSE
PRESS

Contents

COVER PHOTOGRAPH BY ANNE M. EBERHARDT

Introduction

Buying a Thoroughbred at auction can be an exhilarating experience — the fast pace...the competition...the satisfaction of making the winning bid.

Buying at auction also can be intimidating for newcomers to the game. Where do you start? What do you need to know? How can you increase your chances for success?

The Blood-Horse Authoritative Guide to Auctions explains the basics to help prepare newcomers for their first purchase and to refresh veterans about the myriad aspects of horse sales.

A newcomer to the business has a number of options for purchasing a horse at auction. The guide explains the types of sales (e.g., yearling, two-year-olds in training, breeding stock) and when they occur. Information about the major sales companies includes the types of sales they conduct and dates. Maps of the grounds are included.

Other topics address where to get advice, how to apply for credit, and what it means when you sign the sales ticket. Learn why you need to read the fine print and become familiar with each auction company's conditions of sale. Most auction companies operate under the premise of caveat emptor ("buyer beware"), but each company's conditions are different. Some require disclosure of cer-

Buyers contemplate a purchase.

tain medical histories of the horses; others do not. Some will take back a horse for certain reasons; others will not.

This user-friendly guide discusses the roles of consignors, the auctioneer, bid spotters, and others involved in the auction process.

Learn how to work a sale, from inspecting horses to devising a list of candidates and trying to determine price range. Find out why you should consult with a veterinarian before you buy a horse, and why you need to insure a horse as soon as you buy it.

In addition, the guide discusses what horses cost and why and provides a general overview of pedigree and conformation. Also included are a glossary and a reference section as well as interesting statistics such as most expensive horses sold at auction and classic winners sold at auction. Each chapter contains information boxes and useful tips.

The Blood-Horse Authoritative Guide to Auctions is an indispensable tool for newcomers and for anyone who buys horses at auction.

Types of Sales

Buying a horse at public auction for the first time is a rite of passage for prospective horse owners. It's a strange world with its own language and protocol, but with good advisers and, of course, this guide, you should be able to navigate your way through a sale with a certain degree of confidence. Understanding the different types of sales at which you can purchase horses is an important step, but, first, you need to determine at what financial level you can enter horse racing and how quickly you wish to see your purchase on the racetrack, if at all. For example, if you want to race your acquisition immediately, you're not going to find what you need at a yearling sale. The same is true if you're looking for a mare you'd like to breed the following season.

Once you've mulled how much you want to spend and how quickly you want to race or breed, you're ready to find a sale. And to help you choose, below are descriptions of the different types of sales and the estimated time frame in which you can expect your purchase to make it to the track (if racing is your goal).

Yearlings

Yearlings are horses that are one year in age. All Thoroughbreds age one year on January 1, so a horse foaled (born) in 2004 becomes one year old or a yearling on January 1, 2005, regardless of the month the horse was born. Newly turned yearlings can be sold starting in January, but most yearlings are not sent to auction until after mid-July. By that time, yearlings are starting to mature and look less like babies and more like young adults.

For some five and a half decades, the Keeneland July select sale held pride of place as the first yearling sale on the calendar, and for most of that time, it was the best. (Select sales offer horses that meet certain pedigree and conformation criteria as determined by a sales company's selection committee that examine yearlings for an auction. An open sale is just that — open to any horse.) The Keeneland July sale has been the scene of some of the world's most expensive yearling purchases, including the $13.1 million record for Seattle Dancer, a son of Nijinsky II and Triple Crown winner Seattle Slew's dam, My Charmer, purchased at the 1985 auction.

In the late 1990s, the Keeneland September yearling sale, held over a marathon two weeks and offering up to 4,300 youngsters in all price ranges, overtook the July sale in gross receipts, high prices, and

Consigned by Robert E. Courtney/Crestfield Farm LLC, Agent I

Hip No.
164

BAY COLT
Foaled February 18, 2001

Barn
23

BAY COLT

```
                                          ┌ Hail to Reason
                         ┌ Roberto ........┤
          ┌ Kris S. .....┤                 └ Bramalea
          │              │                 ┌ *Princequillo
          │              └ Sharp Queen .....┤
          │                                └ Bridgework
          │                                ┌ Sharpen Up (GB)
          │              ┌ Trempolino ......┤
          └ Najecam .....┤                 └ Trephine (FR)
            (1993)       │                 ┌ *Forli
                         └ Sue Warner ......┤
                                           └ *Bitty Girl
```

By KRIS S. (1977). Stakes winner of $53,350, Bradbury S. Among the lead-
ing sires, sire of 18 crops of racing age, 784 foals, 623 starters, 61 stakes
winners, 465 winners of 1632 races and earning $41,180,906 in N.A., in-
cluding champions Hollywood Wildcat ($1,432,160, Breeders' Cup Dis-
taff **[G1]**, etc.), Soaring Softly ($1,270,433, Breeders' Cup Filly & Mare Turf
[G1], etc.), and of Prized ($2,262,555, Breeders' Cup Turf **[G1]**, etc.),
Kissin Kris **[G1]** ($1,616,936), Brocco **[G1]** ($1,003,550), Kudos **[G1]**.

1st dam
Najecam, by Trempolino. 6 wins, 2 to 5, $175,243, 2nd Princess S. **[G2]**, 3rd
San Clemente H. **[G2]**, Honeymoon H. **[G3]**, Kenneth L. Graf Memorial
H. (RKM, $2,500). Sister to **Lady Ilsley**. Dam of 2 other registered foals,
2 of racing age, including a 2-year-old of 2002, 1 to race--
Gold Ace (c. by Gulch). Placed at 2, 2001 in England.

2nd dam
SUE WARNER, by *Forli. Unraced. Dam of 7 foals, 5 winners, including--
Najecam (f. by Trempolino). Stakes-placed winner, above.
Lady Ilsley (f. by Trempolino). Winner at 2 and 3 in France, 2nd Prix de la
Cochere, 3rd Prix de Lieurey.

3rd dam
*BITTY GIRL, by Habitat. 5 wins at 2 in England, champion 2-year-old filly,
Queen Mary S.-**G2**, Lowther S.-**G3**, Molecomb S.-**G3**, 2nd King's Stand
S.-**G1**; 3 wins at 4, $20,960, in N.A. Sister to **HOT SPARK**. Dam of--
BEAUDELAIRE. 2 wins in 4 starts at 2 in Ireland, Coolmore Try My Best S.,
2nd Coolmore Hello Gorgeous S., etc.; winner in 2 starts at 3 in France,
Prix Maurice de Gheest-**G2**; winner at 3 in England, Beeswing S. Sire.
MEMENTO. Winner at 3 in Ireland, Ballycorus S., 2nd Kilruddery S., etc. Sire.
Nijit. 5 wins, 2 to 4, $96,747, 2nd Ocean City S., Primonetta H.-R, 3rd Co-
tillion S.-**G2**. Dam of 11 foals, 10 to race, 9 winners, including--
SPANISH PARADE. 6 wins at 3, $131,822, Mrs. Revere S. [L] (CD, $37,-
408), etc. Dam of **PARADE QUEEN** (6 wins, $419,357, Mrs. Revere
S. **[G3]**, Joe Namath H. **[G3]**, etc.), **King Namura** (in Japan).
SAVE THE DOE. 2 wins at 3, $57,785, Medusa S. (DET, $16,425), etc.
Size Six. Unraced. Dam of 7 foals to race, 5 winners, including--
LADY SIX. 8 wins, 2 to 4 in Brazil, Grande Premio Euvaldo Lodi **[G3]**, etc.
NEW CAPRICORN. 4 wins, 2 to 4 in England; placed in 2 starts at 3 in
France, 2nd Prix de Pontarme; winner at 4 in Italy, Premio WWF.
Golden Bloomers. 2 wins at 3, $32,705. Dam of **IVY LANE** (3 wins to 3,
2001, $55,610, Emerald Downs H. (HST, $22,932), etc.).
Suffragette. Producer. Granddam of **NOBLE CHALLENGE** (in Australia).
Engagements: NTRA, Breeders' Cup.
Foaled in Kentucky. (KTDF).

KEE 7/02

Catalog page for 2003 champion two-year-old colt Action This Day, who sold as a
yearling at the 2002 Keeneland July sale for $150,000.

importance to both buyer and con-signor. In 2003 the Keeneland July sale was not held due to lack of quality stock and was subsequently taken off the schedule.

Other key yearling sales include the Fasig-Tipton New York sale, pop-ularly known as the "Saratoga sale," held each August; the Fasig-Tipton Kentucky select sale in July and fall sale in October; and Ocala Breeders' Sales' August select sale. Most states that support Thoroughbred racing have a sale that offers yearlings, so you should be able to find a sale near you (see Resource Guide, page 105). Or, you could travel to one of the larger sales, if that fits your budget.

In 2003 the average yearling cost $48,089. Out of 8,843 yearlings

sold that year, 32 sold for a million or more, but the budget-conscious had plenty of options: 4,178 or 47 percent cost $10,000 or less.

Just as with the overall yearling sale numbers, most individual sales will have horses in all price ranges. For example, the 2003 Keeneland September yearling sale's first two days, during which only select youngsters are sold, grossed $131 million for 338 sold with an aver-

ANNE M. EBERHARDT

The Fasig-Tipton Saratoga yearling sale.

LESLIE MARTIN

Buyers can watch "training previews" of two-year-olds in training.

age price of $387,722 and a median of $230,000. Overall, the 12-day sale grossed $273.9 million from 2,968 sold for an average of $92,293 and a median of $34,000. In contrast, the final day grossed just $1.3 million from 173 sold for an average of $7,798 and a median of $5,000.

Many buyers prefer to purchase yearlings later in the year because the young horse has had time to mature and grow a bit more. If a yearling is purchased in the fall, the owner can begin breaking/training lessons to prepare it for a racing career, which usually begins in the spring or summer of the horse's two-year-old year. Yearlings that are

geared toward quick resale in the two-year-olds in training sales also are broken in the late fall/early winter so they can showcase their racing potential for prospective buyers.

Two-year-olds in training

Two-year-olds in training sales consist of horses that turned two on January 1 and are in training, i.e., learning how to breeze and break from the gate, with the hope that they will start racing later that year. This type of sale offers a quicker rate of return for buyers who don't want to wait a year or two to see their investment hit the track.

Many of the two-year-olds entered in these sales are "pinhooks," meaning they were sold as yearlings and are now being resold in expectation of a better price. The hope is that the two-year-old has improved in looks ("filled out") over the winter and shows some speed and talent for running.

Two-year-olds in training sales are held mainly from late winter

THINGSTO**KNOW**

The most prestigious yearling sales take place at Saratoga Springs, New York and in Lexington, Kentucky. Fasig-Tipton's Saratoga sale coincides with racing at that resort town. The Keeneland sale spans up to two weeks in September.

Consigned by Sequel Bloodstock (Becky Thomas), Agent

Barn
1

DARK BAY OR BROWN COLT
Foaled February 14, 1999

Hip No.
72

DARK BAY OR
BROWN COLT

		Skywalker	Relaunch
	Bertrando		Bold Captive
		Gentle Hands	Buffalo Lark
			Three Red Bells
		Septieme Ciel	Seattle Slew
	St. Helens Shadow		Maximova (FR)
	(1993)	Little Bar Fly	Raise a Man
			Splendid Ack Ack

By **BERTRANDO** (1989). Champion older horse, stakes winner of $3,185,-
610, Pacific Classic S. [G1]-ntr, etc. Among the leading sires in California, sire of 5 crops of racing age, 301 foals, 146 starters, 14 stakes
winners, 92 winners of 230 races and earning $7,763,962 in N.A.,
including California champion Smooth Player (to 4, 2000, $760,496,
Lady's Secret Breeders' Cup H. [G2], etc.), and of Cliquot [G3] (4 wins,
$638,260), Here's to You (to 4, 2000, $456,764, Miesque S. [G3], etc.).

1st dam
ST. HELENS SHADOW, by Septieme Ciel. Winner at 2, $54,055, Kachina S.-R
(RUI, $35,836). Dam of 1 named foal of racing age, a 3-year-old of 2001.

2nd dam
LITTLE BAR FLY, by Raise a Man. 3 wins at 2 and 3, $80,150, Vallejo S. [L]
(GG, $20,750). Sister to **SPLENDID ANN**. Dam of 7 winners, including--
  BARFIGHTER (c. by Wild Again). 2 wins at 2, $75,100, Barretts Juvenile
  || S.-R (FPX, $61,380).
  ST. HELENS SHADOW (f. by Septieme Ciel). Stakes winner, above.
  BABY BARFLY (f. by Son of Briartic). 2 wins at 2, $27,717, Mercer Girl S.
  || (YM, $16,848), 2nd Mt. Rainier Sprint Championship S. (YM, $6,084).
  Lush. Winner at 4, 2000, $49,873.
  Blinx Babe. 2 wins at 2, placed at 3, 2000, $45,610.
  Plumb Wild. 2 wins at 3, $42,300.

3rd dam
SPLENDID ACK ACK, by Ack Ack. Winner in 1 start at 3, $4,950. Dam of--
  SPLENDID ANN. 10 wins, 3 to 5 in South Africa, champion older mare
  || twice, Gilbey's S. **[G1]**, Natal Mercury Sprint **[G1]**, South African Fillies
  || Sprint **[G2]**, Southern Cross S. **[G2]**, 2nd Gilbey's Trial **[G3]**, 3rd Mexico
  || Sceptre S. **[G3]**.
  LITTLE BAR FLY. Stakes winner, above.
  She Flaunts It. 4 wins in 8 starts at 3 in France. Producer. Granddam of **First
  Down Dallas** (to 3, 2000, $39,685, 3rd WTBA Lads S. (EMD, $7,155)).

4th dam
SPLENDID SPREE, by Damascus. Unraced. Half-sister to **MANITOULIN** (sire),
  TWICE CITED, **OPEN HEARING**. Dam of 9 foals, 6 winners, including--
  SPLENDID SPRUCE. 5 wins at 2 and 3, $296,500, Santa Anita Derby-**G1**,
  || Will Rogers H.-**G2**, 2nd San Felipe H.-**G2**, Balboa S., 3rd Cinema H.-**G2**.
  SPLENDID WAY. Winner at 3 and 4, Miss Yakima S., 2nd Rhododendron H.
  Complete Warrior. 4 wins at 3 and 5, $52,435, 2nd Olympia S., El Con-
  || quistador S. Sire.
  Rai Den. 3 wins at 3, $117,250.

Engagements: Barretts Juvenile S., Breeders' Cup.
Registered for California-bred owners' premiums.

BAR 3/01

Catalog page for grade I winner Officer, who sold for $700,000 as a two-year-old
at Barretts in 2001.

through the spring and early summer, beginning in February with the Fasig-Tipton Florida select sale and the Ocala Breeders' Sales Co.'s select sale, both at Calder Racecourse in Miami. Other major two-year-olds in training sales include the Barretts select sale in March and the Keeneland sale in April. A few days before a two-year-olds in training sale, the horses will sprint a furlong (eighth of a mile) or two furlongs (a quarter-mile) as fast as they can in "training previews" to showcase their precocity and speed.

In 2003 a total of 3,055 two-year-olds sold at public auction in North America for gross revenue of $139,721,364. The national average price for a two-year-old was $45,735 and the median was $17,000. The Barretts Select sale in 2003 saw a world-record price two-

year-old go through its ring when a colt by Sea of Secrets sold for $2.7 million. (That record was eclipsed in 2004 at the Fasig-Tipton Florida select sale when a Fusaichi Pegasus colt sold for $4.5 million.) The average for the sale was $142,186 from 86 sold with a median of $60,000. The 2003 Fasig-Tipton Florida select sale produced a top price of $1.4 million for a Tale of the Cat colt. The average of $209,187 for 139 sold and median of $150,000 were the highest for any of the major two-year-olds in training sales for the year. At the 2003 OBS Calder sale, a Montbrook colt topped the sale at $1.2 million, while the next highest price was $450,000 for a Polish Numbers filly, a "pinhook" that had brought $57,000 as a yearling. The average for that sale was $108,829 from 117 sold and a median of $75,000.

To get into the breeding side of horse racing, invest in a broodmare.

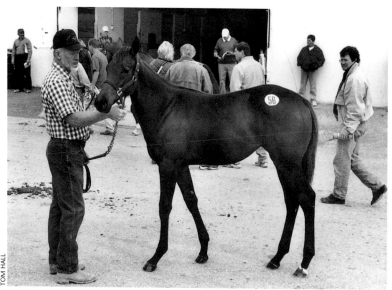

TOM HALL

Weanlings are often pinhooked as yearlings.

Although the 2003 Keeneland sale didn't have a million-dollar two-year-old (the highest price was close at $950,000), it did have a solid average of $167,500 for 128 sold and median of $98,500.

Breeding Stock/Mixed

Breeding stock or mixed sales primarily offer broodmares (mares that have produced offspring) but can include horses of racing age, yearlings, weanlings, broodmare prospects (fillies just off the race-track that have not been bred), and stallions. Mixed sales that include weanlings are limited to the fall. Weanlings are horses that haven't turned one yet and are separated or weaned from their mothers between four and six months of age. A broodmare and her wean-ling colt or filly often will go through the same sale. For persons wanting to invest in the breeding side of the horse business, buying a broodmare is a way to begin. Weanlings are usually purchased

with the intention of reselling them as yearlings. As with buying yearlings, purchasing weanlings requires some ability to see into the future and predict how a weanling is going to develop. This can be tricky, so if you decide to purchase weanlings, be sure to enlist the aid of a horseman who has a proven "eye" for picking young horses.

The leading sale of broodmares and weanlings is the Keeneland November breeding stock sale. Like the Keeneland September yearling auction, the November sale is a two-week marathon comprising all levels of quality in pedigree, con-formation, and appearance. The

> **THINGS**TO**KNOW**
>
> Fillies recently retired from racing, broodmares, and non-pregnant mares make up breeding stock sales. Weanlings also are offered at these sales. The mixed sales are just that — a combination of breeding stock, including stallion prospects and young horses.

15

Consigned by Mill Ridge Sales, Agent

Hip No.
508

WINDSHARP
Dark Bay or Brown Mare; foaled 1991

Barn
11

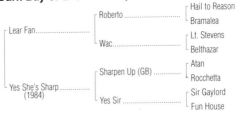

WINDSHARP

```
                                        ┌ Roberto ................... ┌ Hail to Reason
                     ┌ Lear Fan ...........┤                          └ Bramalea
                     │                      └ Wac ..................... ┌ Lt. Stevens
                     │                                                  └ Belthazar
WINDSHARP ──────────┤
                     │                      ┌ Sharpen Up (GB) ........ ┌ Atan
                     └ Yes She's Sharp .....┤                          └ Rocchetta
                         (1984)             └ Yes Sir ................ ┌ Sir Gaylord
                                                                       └ Fun House
```

By LEAR FAN (1981). Stakes winner in England and France, Prix Jacques Le Marois-**G1**, etc. Leading sire in Slovak Republic, sire of 16 crops of racing age, 766 foals, 579 starters, 51 stakes winners, 7 champions, 402 winners of 1308 races and earning $20,775,580/$240,887(CAN) in N.A./U.S. Sire of dams of 30 stakes winners, including champions Sweetest Thing, Collect the Brass, and of Johar, Volga (IRE), Fan Club's Mister, Justenuffheart, Crypto's Redjet, Tzar Rodney (FR), Solar Bound, Big Sky Chester.

1st dam
YES SHE'S SHARP, by Sharpen Up (GB). Winner in 2 starts at 3 in Ireland; winner at 5, $7,595, in N.A./U.S. Sent to Venezuela. Complete race records not available. Dam of 3 registered foals, 3 of racing age, 1 known to race--
  WINDSHARP (f. by Lear Fan). Champion, see record.

2nd dam
YES SIR, by Sir Gaylord. 10 wins, 2 to 5, $89,117, Falls City H., La Troienne S. Set ntr at Churchill Downs. Half-sister to **COURT RULING** (sire), **KING'S PALACE**, **FUNNY CAT**, **GOOD MANNERS**, **FUN PALACE**, **Island Kiss**. Dam of 9 foals, 7 to race, 5 winners, including--
  No Sir (g. by Forward Pass). 10 wins, 2 to 6, $120,611, 2nd Nashua S., etc.
  Jazz Kitty. Winner. Dam of **PURPLE BABE** (f. by J. O. Tobin, $87,685).
RACE RECORD: In France. At 2, unraced; at 3, three wins, once 3rd; at 4, two wins, 3 times 2nd (Grand Prix de Dax Docteur Branere), once 3rd (Grand Prix d'Aquitaine). Totals: 5 wins, 3 times 2nd, twice 3rd. Earned 80,034 euro. In N.A./U.S. At 4, one win (Reloy S. [L] (SA, $43,350)), once 2nd (Long Island H. **[G2]**); at 5, champion grass mare in Canada, champion older mare in Canada, 2 wins (San Luis Rey S. **[G1]**, San Luis Obispo H. **[G2]**), 3 times 2nd (Matriarch S. **[G1]**, San Juan Capistrano Invitational H. **[G1]**, Jockey Club Cup H. [L] (WO, $22,580(CAN))); at 6, three wins (Beverly Hills H. **[G1]**, Santa Ana H. **[G2]**, Estrapade S. [L] (HOL, $63,420)), once 3rd (Santa Barbara H. **[G2]**) in 4 starts. Totals: 6 wins, 4 times 2nd, once 3rd. Earned $1,191,600.
PRODUCE RECORD:
1999 **JOHAR**, c. by Gone West. 5 wins at 3 and 4, 2003, $672,215, Hollywood Derby **[G1]** (HOL, $300,000), Oak Tree Derby **[G2]** (SA, $90,000), San Marcos S. **[G2]** (SA, $90,000), 2nd Del Mar Derby **[G2]** (DMR, $60,000), Will Rogers S. **[G3]** (HOL, $21,300), Oceanside S.-R (DMR, $16,560), 3rd Cinema Breeders' Cup H. **[G3]** (HOL, $25,512).
2000 Dessert, f. by Storm Cat. 2 wins in 4 starts at 3, 2003, $79,560.
2001 Ancient Art, c. by Storm Cat. Unraced.
2002 c. by Fusaichi Pegasus or Anees, died as a weanling; 2003 not pregnant.
Mated to Gone West (Mr. Prospector--Secrettame), last service February 27, 2003. (Believed to be **PREGNANT**).

KEE 11/03

The mare Windsharp sold at the 2003 Keeneland November sale for $6.1 million.

ANNE M. EBERHARDT

Racehorses are sold in horses of racing age sales.

first two days of the sale, although not called the "select" portion of the sale, generally have the highest quality of stock scheduled to pass through the ring. At the 2003 Keeneland sale, a world-record price for a broodmare was set when 1999 Breeders' Cup Juvenile Fillies winner Cash Run sold for $7.1 million. The top weanling at the sale was a colt by Storm Cat and out of Spain who sold for $2.4 million.

In addition to the Keeneland November sale, prospective buyers can find mixed sales throughout the year in all regions of the country, held by state breeders organizations and various sales companies. Keeneland hosts a "horses of all ages" sale in January, where broodmares are sold next to newly turned yearlings. Fasig-Tipton Co. offers mixed sales in Kentucky and Maryland in February and again in December. Barretts and Ocala Breeders' Sales hold mixed sales in October. In North America in 2003, a total of 4,866 broodmares were sold for a gross of $216,248,533, an average of $44,441, and a median of $7,000. The weanling totals for 2003 are 1,728 sold for a gross of $68,058,938, an average of $39,386, and a median of $12,000.

Horses of Racing Age

Two-year-olds in training sales are technically "horses of racing age" sales because racehorses begin racing at that age. However, a few auctions also include older racehorses (ages three and up) in their catalogs. If, as a prospective buyer, you want instant gratification, this is the type of sale to attend. It is the equivalent of buying a racehorse privately or claiming a horse from a race, but in a more formalized set-

17

ting. Some of the horses in a horses of racing age sale may not have raced yet, as is the case with many two-year-olds, even in the fall. These horses might be unraced because of minor injuries received in training or their owners might not have deemed the horses mature enough physically and/or mentally to race. You should have a trainer, preferably one familiar with the horses in the sale and their training and/or racing efforts, to help you evaluate them. (See Ch. 4, Auction Experts.) The main horses of racing age sale is conducted by Fasig-Tipton Co. at the end of October at Belmont Park in New York. A small, one-day sale, it offers a mix of established racehorses and unraced horses in training. Past performances, such as those found in the *Daily Racing Form*, are included as an appendix for horses with race records, although each horse's record is included on the catalog page. This type of sale can be a place to find bargains. The 2003 Fasig-Tipton New York horses of racing age sale grossed $449,400 for 55 sold, with an average of $8,171, and a median of $4,700.

Stallion seasons and shares

Stallions that are standing at stud rarely go through the auction ring, usually being syndicated or sold privately. On occasion, a few stallions will be sold at a mixed sale, usually as part of a dispersal or to dissolve a partnership.

For breeders interested in acquiring seasons (the right to breed a mare to a stallion in one particular year) or shares (the right to breed a mare to a stallion for every year of his breeding life), a few auctions are devoted to these stallion seasons/shares. Fasig-Tipton hosts one in February and another, its "Stallion Access Champagne Sale," in August in conjunction with its Saratoga yearling sale.

Seasons and shares are usually sold "no guarantee," meaning even if a live foal does not result from the mating, you are out the amount you paid. However, you can obtain insurance on no guarantee seasons under certain conditions (e.g. the age and/or fertility of the stallion) so if you are interested in this type of season, contact an equine insurance agent. Sometimes a stallion season will be sold with a limited warranty, usually in the case of an older stallion that may be nearing retirement.

At the 2003 Stallion Access sale, no-guarantee seasons for 2004 to top sire Seeking the Gold went for $100,000 and $125,000. Seeking the Gold had a 2003 stud fee of $225,000 live foal, but he stands for $150,000 in 2004. (A stud fee with a "live foal" designation generally means that if there is no live foal, there is no stud fee to be paid; however, stud fees often are required to be paid in the fall of the year bred and then are refunded if no live foal is produced.) Stallion seasons/shares sales can be good indicators of stallions' stud fees for the coming year. At the same sale, a share in Distorted Humor (sire of 2003 Kentucky Derby and Preakness Stakes winner Funny Cide) sold for $500,000 and a season sold for $40,000. Distorted Humor's 2004 stud fee is $50,000.

—*Judy L. Marchman*

2

Major Sales Companies

More than twenty auction companies hold Thoroughbred sales each year. The largest and most well known are Keeneland and Fasig-Tipton, both based in Kentucky; Ocala Breeders' Sales in Florida; and Barretts in California. State breeders' associations run many of the smaller, more regional sales, almost all of them in close proximity to a racetrack. A list of U.S. and Canadian auction companies and the types of Thoroughbred sales they hold each year is included in the Resource Guide at the back of this book.

Most of the sales are mixed (a combination of broodmares, weanlings, yearlings, and two-year-olds), though in recent years, two-year-olds in training sales have become more widespread. Unable to compete with Kentucky's deep-rooted position as the nation's Thoroughbred breeding center, regional sales companies — particularly in Florida and California — have found their forte selling two-year-olds. The trend started in the early 1950s when Joe O'Farrell, the founder of Ocala Stud, and Humphrey Finney of Fasig-Tipton, put on the first two-year-olds in training sale in Hialeah, Florida. The state's mild winters permitted year-round training and the sales provided a supply of young athletes, while south Florida's popularity with the East Coast's racing elite provided the marketplace to sell them. The concept grew quickly. The two-year-olds in training sales market has grown from that single winter sale at Hialeah Park in the early 1950s to more than fifteen sales nationwide in 2002, many of which are in Florida and California.

Despite the growth of two-year-old sales, tradition reigns heavy in the world of horse sales. Keeneland and Fasig-Tipton are the most established sales companies and hold the most well attended equine auctions in the world. Keeneland runs its sales in the Bluegrass of Kentucky, the epicenter of breeding, and Fasig-Tipton has also made Lexington its home base while maintaining other sites along the East Coast and in Texas.

ANNE M. EBERHARDT

Keeneland's sales grounds.

19

Keeneland

Keeneland Association
4201 Versailles Road
P.O. Box 1690
Lexington, KY 40588
(859) 254-3412
E-mail: sales@keeneland.com
www.keeneland.com

MIXED
January

TWO-YEAR-OLDS IN TRAINING
April

YEARLING
September

BREEDING STOCK
November

Keeneland is where horse owners come to buy quality Thoroughbred racehorses (or future racehorses). At

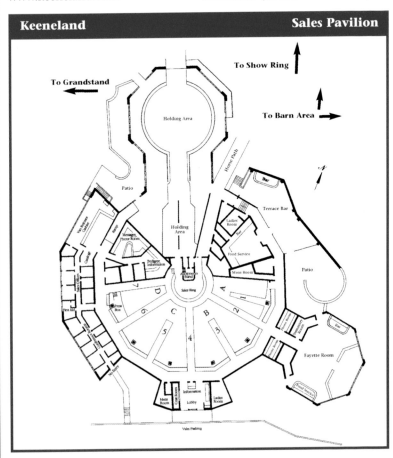

Keeneland — Sales Grounds

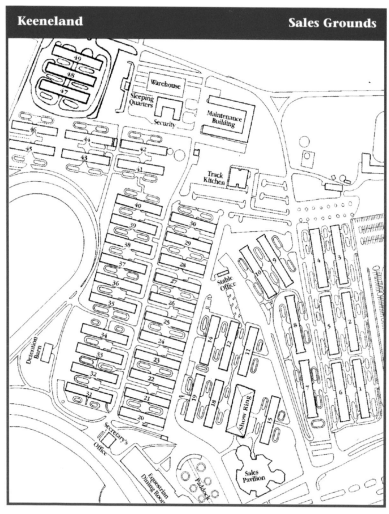

any one of its four annual sales, it would not be surprising to find represented all of the world's continents, with the exception of the one too frigid for horse racing. And how does one become and remain the world's purveyor of racehorses? Well, geography — it helps to be in the heart of horse country. It also takes an adherence to quality and a willingness to forge foreign relationships. Throw in some unforeseen circumstances and the pixels come together.

A wartime gas shortage in 1943 prevented Kentucky breeders from sending their yearlings to Saratoga Springs, New York, so Fasig-Tipton transplanted the sale to Keeneland racecourse in Lexington. A year later, after a dispute with the Kentucky breeders, Fasig-Tipton elected not to hold the sale at Keeneland, a decision that prompted the formation of the Breeders' Sales Company.

From the very beginning the sales focused on quality, with 1945 Kentucky Derby winner Hoop, Jr.

coming from the first sale and the champion two-year-old filly Beaugay and the champion two-year-old colt Star Pilot products of the second sale. Through the years a few more sales were added, and the Breeders' Sales Company eventually came under Keeneland's aegis.

In the mid-1960s Vincent O'Brien's success with Keeneland graduates in European races enticed more international buyers to its sales and heightened its reputation. The discovery of oil in the Persian Gulf in the late 1970s brought the Maktoums, the ruling family of Dubai, into the bidding ring. With advantageous tax laws at the time, Americans also joined the fray. Records were set in every category as bidding reached the million-dollar mark and kept on going. In 1978 and 1979, two sons of Northern Dancer — champions Nureyev and Storm Bird, respectively — were bought for $1 million or more. Two more Northern Dancer colts each brought more than $3 million in 1981. BBA Ireland bought Ballydoyle (a full brother to Storm Bird) for the Robert Sangster group, while the Aston Upthorpe group of Sheikh Mohammed bin Rashid al Maktoum bought Shareef Dancer. Staggering prices followed the next few years, including $13.1 million for Seattle Dancer (a grandson of Northern Dancer and a half brother to 1977 Triple Crown winner Seattle Slew) in 1985.

Today Keeneland holds a mixed sale in January, a two-year-olds in training sale in April, a yearling sale in September, and a breeding stock sale in November. The sales have been so successful that Keeneland has been able to supplement its purses during its race meets to attract some of the finest names in horse racing. At the November 2003 breeding stock sale, the median price was $32,000, equaling the record set in 1999. Additionally, a record price for a broodmare was set when Cash Run, a daughter of Seeking the Gold who had won the 1999 Breeders' Cup Juvenile Fillies, sold for $7.1 million.

Where to Stay

Comfort Suites
Beaumont Centre
3070 Fieldstone Way, Lexington
(800) 228-5150

Courtyard by Marriott
775 Newtown Ct., Lexington
(800) 321-2211

Embassy Suites
1801 Newtown Pike, Lexington
(800) EMBASSY

Hilton Suites
245 Lexington Green Cir.
Lexington
(800) 367-4754

Hyatt Regency
401 W. High St., Lexington
(800) 233-1234

Marriott's Griffin Gate Resort
1800 Newtown Pike, Lexington
(800) 228-9290

Radisson Plaza
369 W. Vine St., Lexington
(800) 333-3333

Wyndham Garden Hotel
1938 Stanton Way, Lexington
(800) WYNDHAM

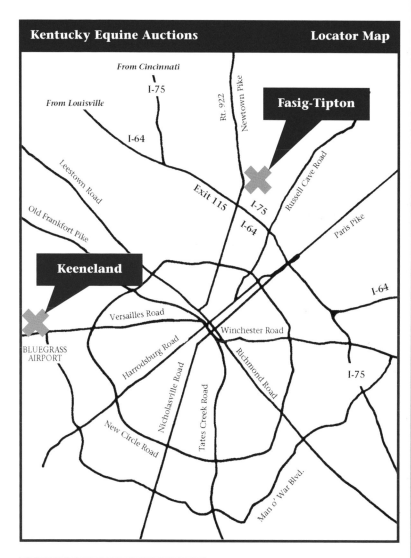

Kentucky Equine Auctions — **Locator Map**

Where to Eat

a la lucie
159 N. Limestone St.,
Lexington
(859) 252-5277

Bistro La Belle
121 E. Main St., Midway
(859) 846-4233

deSha's
101 N. Broadway, Lexington
(859) 259-3771

Dudley's
380 S. Mill St., Lexington
(859) 252-1010

Furlong's
E. Main St. & S. Ashland
Lexington
(859) 266-9000

Malone's
3347 Tates Creek Rd., Lexington
(859) 335-6500

Merrick Inn
3380 Tates Creek Rd., Lexington
(859) 269-5417

Nadine's
Palomar Centre, Lexington
(859) 223-0797

Portofino
249 E. Main St., Lexington
(859) 253-9300

(For more hotel and restaurant selections, see the Keeneland sales catalog or contact the Lexington Convention & Visitors Bureau at 800-845-3959 or go to www.visitlex.com.)

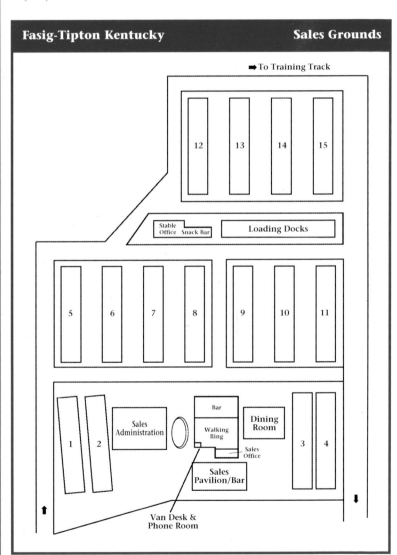

Fasig-Tipton Kentucky — **Sales Grounds**

➡ To Training Track

12 13 14 15

Stable Office   Snack Bar   Loading Docks

5 6 7 8   9 10 11

1 2   Sales Administration   Bar   Dining Room   3 4
Walking Ring
Sales Office
Sales Pavilion/Bar

Van Desk & Phone Room

Fasig-Tipton

Fasig-Tipton is the oldest and most widespread Thoroughbred auction company in North America, with operations in Florida, New York, Texas, Maryland, and its home office in Kentucky.

William B. Fasig and Edward A. Tipton incorporated the company in 1898, originally starting out selling Thoroughbreds, show horses, and Standardbreds in New York City's Madison Square Garden and later at Belmont Park on Long Island. The company had a monopoly on the Thoroughbred auction business until World War II when an embargo on the shipment of non-essential goods prevented Kentucky breeders from sending their horses to New York for Fasig-Tipton's Saratoga yearling sale. Fasig-Tipton brought the sale to Kentucky, but a dispute led Kentucky breeders to form their own cooperative that would later become the Keeneland

ANNE M. EBERHARDT

Fasig-Tipton Kentucky sales arena.

Association and Fasig-Tipton's primary competition.

Fasig-Tipton has a long tradition of selling champions, particularly at Saratoga, starting in 1918 with the great Man o' War. Many other yearlings from the Saratoga sales have also gone on to become part of racing and breeding history, such as Raise a Native, Natalma (the dam of Northern Dancer), Hoist the Flag, Danzig, Miswaki, Conquistador Cielo, and 1991 Horse of the Year Black Tie Affair.

Three more recent standouts who found their owners in the Saratoga sales ring are 1993 Belmont Stakes winner Colonial Affair, 1994 Kentucky Derby winner Go for Gin, and 2002 champion two-year-old male Vindication.

Periodically conducting dispersals and special auctions in Kentucky, Fasig-Tipton established a permanent, full-service office in Lexington in 1972 and began a year-round sales schedule that includes all categories of Thoroughbreds.

The Kentucky division has produced its own share of winners, including classic-winning graduates such as Seattle Slew, Genuine Risk, Dancing Brave, and Rainbow Quest. More recent Kentucky division sales graduates are two-time champion filly Silverbulletday and 2001 Dubai World Cup winner Captain Steve.

The company also auctions stallion shares and seasons.

Fasig-Tipton Company
2400 Newtown Pike
P.O. Box 13610
Lexington, KY 40583
(859) 255-1555
E-mail: info@fasigtipton.com
www.fasigtipton.com

MIXED
February, Fasig-Tipton Kentucky, Lexington, Ky.
(in conjunction with the Stallion Access Sale of Select Seasons and Shares held immediately afterward)

SELECT YEARLINGS
July, Fasig-Tipton Kentucky, Lexington, Ky.

YEARLINGS
October, Fasig-Tipton Kentucky, Lexington, Ky.

MIXED (Adena Springs)
November, Fasig-Tipton Kentucky, Lexington, Ky.

SELECT MIXED
November, Fasig-Tipton Kentucky, Lexington, Ky.

STALLION SELECT SEASONS AND SHARES
November, Fasig-Tipton Kentucky, Lexington, Ky.

Fasig-Tipton Florida (Calder)

Fasig-Tipton Florida
21001 N.W. 27th Ave.
Miami, FL 33056
(305) 626-3947

SELECT TWO-YEAR-OLDS IN TRAINING
February, Fasig-Tipton Florida, Calder Race Course, Miami

Where to Stay

Calder Holiday Inn
21485 NW 27th Ave., Miami
(305) 621-5801

Don Shula's Hotel & Golf Club
7601 Miami Lakes Dr.,
Miami Lakes
(305) 821-1150

Doral Golf Resort & Spa
4400 NW 87th Ave., Miami
(305) 592-2000

Fontainebleau
4441 Collins Ave., Miami
(305) 538-2000

Wyndham Hotel
1601 Biscayne Blvd., Miami
(305) 374-0000

Where to Eat

Big Tomato Market Grill
8300 Pines Blvd., Pembroke Pines
(954) 704-0100

Christine Lee's
17082 Collins Ave., Miami
(305) 947-1717

Las Brisas Restaurant
600 N. Surf Rd., Hollywood
(954) 923-1500

Fasig-Tipton Florida (Calder)   **Locator Map**

Martha's
6024 N. Ocean Dr., Hollywood
(954) 923-5444

Tropical Acres
2500 Griffin Rd., Ft. Lauderdale
(954) 989-2500

(For more hotel and restaurant selections, see the Fasig-Tipton Florida sales catalog or visit Calder Race Course's web site at www.calderracecourse.com.)

Calder Race Course hosts sales for Fasig-Tipton and Ocala Breeders' Sales.

Fasig-Tipton Midlantic

Fasig-Tipton Midlantic
356 Fair Hill Drive, Suite C
Elkton, MD 21921
(410) 392-5555

MIXED
February, Fasig-Tipton Midlantic,
Timonium, Md.

TWO-YEAR-OLDS IN TRAINING
May, Fasig-Tipton Midlantic,
Timonium, Md.

**TWO-YEAR-OLDS IN TRAINING
AND HORSES OF RACING AGE**
July, Fasig-Tipton Midlantic,
Timonium, Md. (not held in 2004)

YEARLINGS
late September/early October
Fasig-Tipton Midlantic, Timonium,
Md.

MIXED
December, Fasig-Tipton Midlantic,
Timonium, Md.

Where to Stay

Days Hotel & Conference Center
9615 Deereco Rd., Timonium
(410) 560-1000

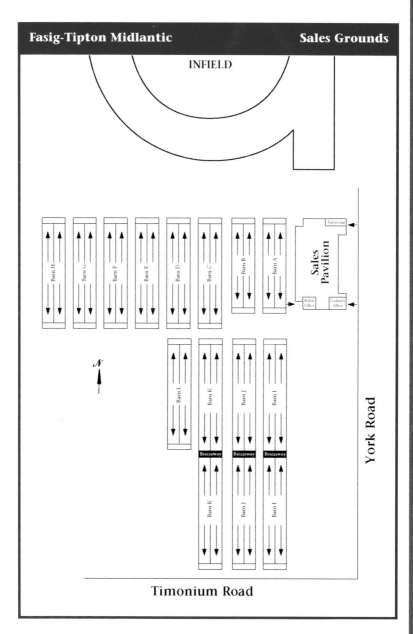

Embassy Suites
213 International Cir., Hunt Valley
(410) 584-1400

Hampton Inn
11200 York Rd., Hunt Valley
(410) 527-1500

Marriott Hunt Valley Inn
245 Shawan Rd., Hunt Valley
(410) 785-7000

Red Roof Inn Baltimore North
111 W Timonium Rd., Timonium
(410) 666-0380

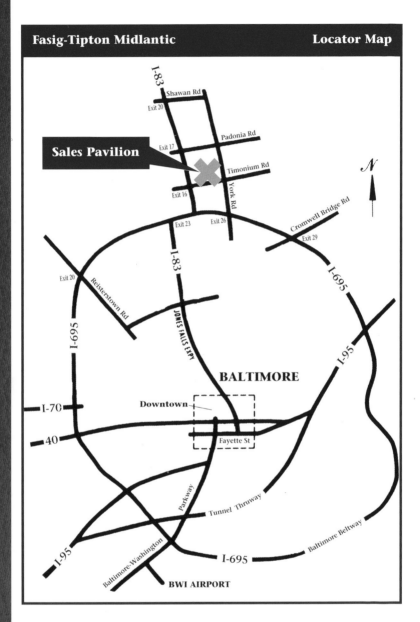

Fasig-Tipton Midlantic — Locator Map

Where to Eat

Bo Brooks at Lighthouse Point
2780-A Lighthouse Point,
Baltimore
(410) 558-0202

Cinnamon Tree Restaurant
Marriott Hunt Valley Inn
(410) 785-7000

**Dulaney Steak & Seafood
Restaurant**
903 Dulaney Valley Rd., Towson
(410) 321-7400

McCormick & Schmick's
Seafood Restaurant
  711 Eastern Ave., Baltimore
  (410) 234-1300

Shula's Steakhouse
  101 W. Fayette St., Baltimore
  (410) 385-6604

Michael's
  2119 York Rd., Timonium
  (410) 252-2022

(For more hotel and restaurant selections, see the Fasig-Tipton Midlantic sales catalog or visit the Baltimore Convention & Visitors Bureau's web site at www.baltimore.org.)

Fasig-Tipton New York

Fasig-Tipton New York
40 Elmont Road
Elmont, NY 11003
(516) 328-1800

SELECT YEARLINGS
August, Fasig-Tipton New York,
Saratoga Springs, N.Y.

STALLION SELECT
SEASONS AND SHARES
August, Fasig-Tipton New York,
Saratoga Springs, N.Y.

PREFERRED YEARLINGS
August, Fasig-Tipton New York,
Saratoga Springs, N.Y.

HORSES OF RACING AGE
October, Fasig-Tipton New York,
Belmont Park,
Elmont, N.Y.

Where to Stay (Saratoga)

Hilton Garden Inn
  125 S. Broadway, Saratoga
  (518) 587-1500

The Inn at Saratoga
  231 Broadway, Saratoga
  (800) 274-3573

Prime Hotel & Resort
  534 Broadway, Saratoga
  (518) 584-4000

The Roosevelt Inn & Suites
  177 S. Broadway, Saratoga
  (518) 584-0980

Where to Stay (Long Island)

Garden City Hotel
  45 Seventh St., Garden City
  (516) 747-3000

Holiday Inn Rockville Centre
  173 Sunrise Hwy., Rockville Centre
  (516) 678-1300

Long Island Marriott
  101 James Doolittle Blvd., Uniondale
  (516) 794-3800

Wingate Inn
  821 Stewart Ave., Garden City
  (516) 705-9000

Where to Eat (Saratoga)

The Parting Glass
  40-42 Lake Ave., Saratoga
  (518) 583-1916

31

Fasig-Tipton New York (Saratoga)   Sales Grounds

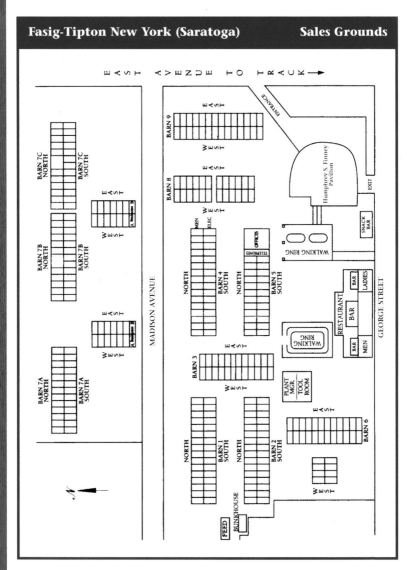

Professor Moriarity's
 430 Broadway, Saratoga
 (518) 587-5981

Siro's
 168 Lincoln Ave. Saratoga
 (518) 584-4030

The Wishing Well
 744 Saratoga Rd., Gansevoort
 (518) 584-7640

Where to Eat (Long Island)

Burton & Doyle Steakhouse
 661 Northern Blvd., Great Neck
 (516) 487-9200

Jameson's Bar & Grill
 157 Tulip Ave., Floral Park
 (516) 326-8300

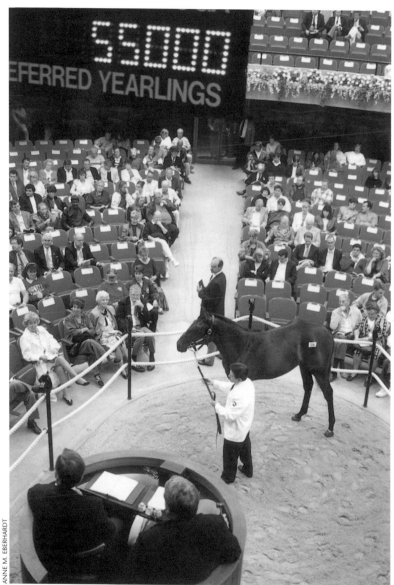

Fasig-Tipton Saratoga sales pavilion.

Papa Razzi Trattoria
1500 Jericho Turnpike, Westbury
(516) 877-7744

Stillwaters
2851 Ocean Ave., Seaford
(516) 783-1999

(For more hotel and restaurant selections, visit the Saratoga Springs Convention & Tourism Bureau's web site at www.discoversaratoga.com and the Long Island Convention & Tourism Bureau at www.licvb.com.)

33

Fasig-Tipton Texas

Fasig-Tipton Texas
1000 Lone Star Parkway
Grand Prairie, TX 75050
(972) 262-0000

TWO-YEAR-OLDS IN TRAINING
March, Fasig-Tipton Texas,
Lone Star Park,
Grand Prairie, Texas

YEARLINGS
August, Fasig-Tipton Texas, Lone
Start Park, Grand Prairie, Texas

MIXED
December, Fasig-Tipton Texas,
Lone Star Park, Grand Prairie, Texas

Where to Stay

Arlington Hilton
2401 E. Lamar Blvd., Arlington
(817) 640-3322

Comfort Suites
2075 N. Hwy. 360, Grand Prairie
(817) 633-6311

Country Suites by Carlson
1075 Wet-N-Wild Way, Arlington
(817) 261-8900

Doubletree Hotel
4650 W. Airport Frwy., Irving
(972) 790-0093

Fairfield Inn
E. Lamar Blvd., Arlington
(817) 649-5800

Four Seasons Resort & Club
4150 N. MacArthur Blvd., Irving
(972) 717-2533

Hampton Inn
2050 N. Hwy. 360, Grand Prairie
(972) 988-8989

Homegate Studio/Suites
1108 N. Hwy. 360, Grand Prairie
(972) 975-0000

Hyatt Regency
DFW Airport, Irving
(972) 453-1234

Omni Mandalay Hotel
221 E. Las Colinas Blvd., Irving
(972) 556-0800

Where to Eat

El Fenix
4608 S. Cooper St., Arlington
(817) 557-4309

Mi Pueblo Mexican Restaurant & Bakery
414 E. Main St., Grand Prairie
(972) 642-1237

Real Pit Barbecue
700 S. Belt Line Rd., Grand Prairie
(972) 264-3820

Texas Land & Cattle Co.
2009-E Copeland Rd., Arlington
(817) 461-1500

Trail Dust Steak House
2300 E. Lamar Blvd., Arlington
(817) 640-6411

*(For more hotel and restaurant selections,
contact the Grand Prairie Convention &
Visitors Bureau at www.gptexas.com.
or the Arlington Convention & Visitors
Bureau at www.arlington.org.)*

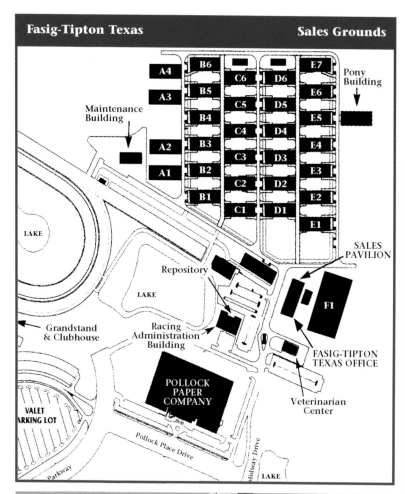

Fasig-Tipton Texas — Sales Grounds

Pony Building

Maintenance Building

A4 A3 A2 A1

B6 B5 B4 B3 B2 B1

C6 C5 C4 C3 C2 C1

D6 D5 D4 D3 D2 D1

E7 E6 E5 E4 E3 E2 E1

SALES PAVILION

Repository

LAKE

LAKE

Grandstand & Clubhouse

Racing Administration Building

F1

FASIG-TIPTON TEXAS OFFICE

POLLOCK PAPER COMPANY

Veterinarian Center

VALET PARKING LOT

Pollock Place Drive

Midway Drive

Parkway

LAKE

Fasig-Tipton's Texas office is based at Lone Star Park.

SKIP DICKSTEIN

35

Ocala Breeders' Sales Company

Ocala Breeders' Sales Company
1701 S.W. 60th Ave.
P.O. Box 99
Ocala, FL 34478
(352) 237-2154
E-mail: obs@obssales.com
www.obssales.com

MIXED
January, Ocala Breeders' Sales
Company, Ocala, Fla.

SELECT TWO-YEAR-OLDS
February, Calder Race Course, Miami

SELECT TWO-YEAR-OLDS
March, Ocala Breeders' Sales
Company

TWO-YEAR-OLDS
April, Ocala Breeders' Sales
Company

**TWO-YEAR-OLDS AND
HORSES OF RACING AGE**
June, Ocala Breeders' Sales
Company

YEARLINGS
August, Ocala Breeders' Sales
Company

MIXED
October, Ocala Breeders' Sales
Company

ANNE M. EBERHARDT

The Ocala sales pavilion.

Ocala Breeders' Sales Company — Locator Map

A group of twenty-five Florida horsemen formed Ocala Breeders' Sales (OBS) in 1974 after they were unable to convince the Florida Breeders' Sales Company (whose sales were conducted by Fasig-Tipton in Ocala and at Hialeah Park in Miami) to build a suitable sales facility in Ocala. OBS held its first sale in its new pavilion in January of 1975 and has been going strong ever since, including absorbing the Florida Breeders' Sales Company in the early 1980s. OBS currently holds seven sales a year, the most well attended being its select two-year-olds in training sale at Calder Race Course in February and its March select two-year-olds in training sale at the OBS facility on Airport Road in Ocala.

OBS also holds a winter mixed sale in January, a two-year-olds in training sale in April, a two-year-olds and horses of racing age sale in June, a select and open yearling sale in August, and a fall mixed sale in October. The sales company also hosts a one-day race meet at its training center in March, leading up to the select two-year-olds in training sale. This "Championship Stakes Day" helps promote OBS sales graduates and Florida-breds. There is no wagering on the races, though the sales company does offer inter-track betting at its on-site simulcast parlor.

Since OBS' inception its credo has been value for the money. The pedigrees might not be as prestigious as those found at the Keeneland and

37

Saratoga sales, but quality horses can be found among its ranks. Silver Charm, winner of the 1997 Kentucky Derby and Preakness, and 1998 Horse of the Year Skip Away are both OBS graduates.

"It's a great place to buy a great athlete at a good price," said Jay Friedman, who does marketing and publicity for OBS.

Many of the two-year-olds sales are dominated by pinhookers who bought their stock at the Keeneland yearling sale the previous September. Many of the horses are sold for racing overseas, especially in Korea, with some of the more modest pedigrees being sold to clients from South America, Friedman said.

Where to Stay

Best Western
Ocala Park Centre
I-75 and State Rd. 200, Ocala
(800) 704-0849

Comfort Inn
I-75 and State Rd. 40, Ocala
(800) 221-2222

Fairfield Inn
I-75 and State Rd. 40, Ocala
(800) 228-2800

Hampton Inn
3434 SW College Road, Ocala
(800) 854-3205

Hilton Hotel
I-75 and State Rd. 200, Ocala
(800) 445-8667

La Quinta Inn & Suites
I-75 and State Rd. 200, Ocala
(800) NuRooms

Quality Inn
I-75 and State Rd. 40, Ocala
(352) 629-0381

Steinbrenner's Ramada Yankee Inn
I-75 and State Rd. 27, Ocala
(800) 800-8000

Where to Eat

Carmichael's Restaurant
3105 E. Silver Springs Blvd., Ocala
(352) 622-3636

Crispers Restaurant
2604 SW 19th Ave. #102, Ocala
(352) 622-4819

Harry's Seafood Bar & Grill
24 SE 1st Ave., Ocala
(352) 840-0900

Kotobuki Japanese Steak House
2463 SW 27th Ave., Ocala
(352) 237-3900

Palace of India
506 S. Pine Ave., Ocala
(352) 369-1040

(For more hotels and restaurants, contact the Ocala/Marion County Chamber of Commerce at 352-629-8051 or visit ocalacc.com.)

Barretts

Barretts

Barretts Equine Ltd.
P.O. Box 2010
Pomona, CA 91769
(909) 629-3099
E-mail: barrettseq@aol.com
www.barretts.com

MIXED
January, Fairplex Park,
Pomona, Calif.

SELECT TWO-YEAR-OLDS IN TRAINING
March, Fairplex Park

TWO-YEAR-OLDS
May, Fairplex Park

TWO-YEAR-OLD AND HORSES OF RACING AGE
June (starting 2004), Fairplex Park

PREFERRED YEARLINGS
early October, Fairplex Park

MIXED
late October, Fairplex Park

STIDHAM & ASSOCIATES

A two-year-old sells at Barretts.

When the old sales pavilion at Hollywood Park was torn down in 1984 to lengthen the track for the inaugural Breeders' Cup, no one rushed to build a replacement. California Thoroughbred Sales, sales arm of the California Thoroughbred Breeders' Association, instead continued its sales in a parking-lot tent at Hollywood Park. After a few years of this, horseman and developer Fred Sahadi had had enough and went into action. He partnered with the Los Angeles County Fair Association and built a $13 million Thoroughbred auction complex on the Fairplex Park racetrack grounds, just 15 miles east of Santa Anita racetrack. Sahadi named the sales company Barretts, after his son Stephen, whose middle name is Barrett.

Barretts held its inaugural sale in March of 1990 and now is the only California equine auction company to hold a full calendar of sales. Its niche is two-year-olds in training. Barretts holds a mixed sale in January, a select two-year-olds in training sale in March, a two-year-olds sale in May, a preferred yearling sale in early October, and a mixed sale in late October. In 2004 Barretts added a two-year-olds in training and horses of racing age sale in June.

Barretts president Gerald McMahon said Barretts has become a source for starters at the California racetracks, where field sizes have traditionally been small. Many colts that have come out of the sales have gone on to become successful racehorses and sires, including Unbridled's Song, Honour and Glory, and Kissin Kris.

"Our operation is not as well known as those in Kentucky, New York, or Florida, but we operate at that level," McMahon said. "We attract major names and buyers but also serve the smaller breeding industry on the West Coast."

Barretts

Where to Stay

Doubletree Hotel
222 N. Vineyard Ave., Ontario
(909) 983-0909

Embassy Suites
211 E. Huntington Dr., Arcadia
(626) 445-8525

Marriott Ontario Airport Hotel
2200 E. Holt Blvd., Ontario
(909) 975-5000

Sheraton Suites — Fairplex
601 W. McKinley, Pomona
(909) 622-2220

Locator Map

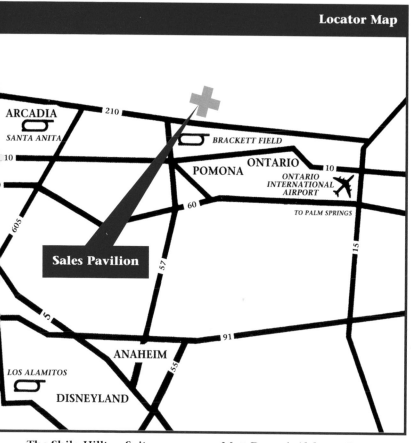

The Shilo Hilltop Suites
3101 Temple Ave., Pomona
(909) 598-7666

The Shilo Hotel
3200 Temple Ave., Pomona
(909) 598-0073

Where to Eat

Bistro 45
45 S. Mentor Ave., Pasadena
(626) 795-2478

Casa del Rey
1220 S. Baldwin Ave., Arcadia
(626) 446-8537

Matt Denny's Alehouse Restaurant
145 E. Huntington Dr., Arcadia
(626) 446-1077

Rosa's Beyond Italian
425 N. Vineyard Ave., Ontario
(909) 937-1220

Twin Palms
101 West Green St., Pasadena
(626) 577-2567

(For more hotel and restaurant selections, see the Barretts sales catalog or call the Pomona Chamber of Commerce at 909-622-1256.)

41

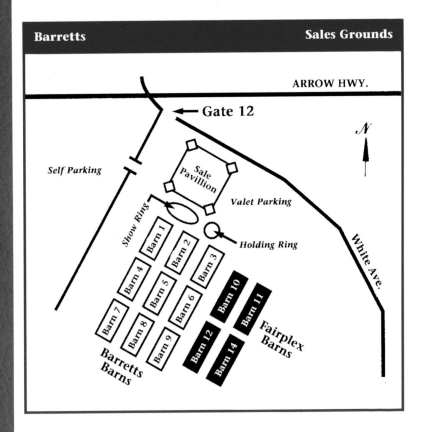

3

How Sales Work

Buying at auction requires more than just showing up, finding a horse you like, and making a bid. New buyers need to do their homework, which ranges from introducing yourself to auction company officials to understanding the conditions under which horses are sold. New buyers also need to learn the protocols of participating in an auction. The following section covers some of the key areas of the auction process.

Credit Application

The sales company collects payment on behalf of consignors. A variety of payment methods are accepted, from cold cash to credit cards (up to $5,000 in purchases can be made on plastic at Barretts), including personal check, company check, cashier's check, traveler's check, or wire transfer. But even if you bring a valise packed with greenbacks, it's best to register with the sales office before you bid and notify them of how you intend to pay. A credit application form, or as some sales companies are now calling it, a buyer registration form, can be found at the front of the sales catalog or on some companies' web sites, from which you can print it out and mail it back. Provide your billing address, name and address of your bank, account number, the name of a bank officer the sales company can contact, and the amount of money you expect to bid, so the sales company can do a credit check on you.

Credit approval can take anywhere from a half hour to a couple of days, depending entirely on the information you supply and how cooperative your bank is. The right way to obtain approval is to send in

a credit application a couple of weeks in advance. If you show up to the sale without approved credit, you'll have to fill out a lot of detailed credit information first, and wait.

When you register as a buyer, notify your bank that the sales company will be contacting it to check your credit standing. When you arrive at the sales grounds, you should check in with the sales

> **THINGS TO KNOW**
>
> Most major sales companies make their catalogs and sales results available online. Check the Resource Guide for sales company web addresses.

office before you bid, to be sure you have been approved.

Sales companies will allow you a 15-day grace period to settle up on your purchases. The industry refers to it as credit, but it is actually a payment extension rather than a credit transaction.

Conditions of Sale

When your catalog arrives, you'll want to jump right in on the pages of horses being offered. But take a moment to read those pages you skipped at the beginning of the book. The conditions of sale are not as much fun as the pedigrees, but you should be familiar with them before you bid.

Buying a Thoroughbred at auc-tion is a commercial transaction, not a consumer transaction. In the Thoroughbred business, the buyer, seller, and sales company are bound by the conditions of sale

---

Buyer Registration Form

Complete this section to register to bid:

Purchases will be made in the name of_____

Name of responsible party (if other than above) _____

_____

Billing Address:

_____

_____

_____

Method of Payment
_____Personal Check _____Wire Transfer
_____Company Check _____Travelers Checks
_____Cashiers Check

SSN _____or Int'l Drivers No. _____

or Passport No._____

Telephones:

Home _____Office_____

Mobile_____Fax_____

Email address _____

Expected Amount of Purchases $ _____

This section to be completed if you wish to be invoiced for your purchases. Payment is due 15 days after the last day of the sale. If you do not wish to be invoiced, payment is expected within 30 minutes of the fall of the hammer. The financial institution that you list below will be contacted concerning your request for credit. Please advise them.

Financial Information

Name of Institution _____

Address _____

_____

_____

Telephone No. _____Fax Number _____

Account No. _____

Officer to be Contacted _____

By signing this form applicant and/or responsible party authorizes Keeneland Association, Inc. to perform a credit investigation and if the applicant is not an indi-vidual, the undersigned individual agrees to be personally responsible to Keeneland for payment of the applicant's account pursuant to the Conditions of Sale.

Signature of Applicant/Responsible Party

Example of a buyer registration form.

printed in the front of the catalog. Conditions of sale are the rules and regulations that cover business ranging from extension of credit to resolution of bidding disputes and other particulars. They also spell out any limited warranties that might apply to physical defects of horses, including when a buyer can return a horse that turned out

Conditions of This Sale

IMPORTANT NOTICES. PLEASE READ.

This sale is governed by these Conditions of Sale and all announcements from the auctioneer's stand or otherwise ("Announcements"). All sellers, consignors, agents, owners, prospective bidders/buyers, all other interested parties and all sales are bound by and subject to the provisions of the Conditions of Sale as set forth in this catalogue and Announcements.

All prospective bidders are urged to **carefully examine horses** in which they may be interested personally and/or by agents or veterinarians of their choosing **BEFORE bidding** as they are accepting any horse purchased with all conditions and defects except those conditions and defects which are specifically warranted in these Conditions of Sale and were not so announced prior to sale.

Conditions revealed by post-sale laryngoscopic examinations for which rescission is allowed are **ONLY** as set forth in Condition of Sale Sixth. There are other conditions which may be revealed by that examination or other examinations which may affect the desirability of purchasing the horse but which **are not grounds** for rescission of sale.

Consignors may make written arrangements with prospective bidder/buyers prior to sale which differ from these Conditions. In such event, Keeneland shall have no responsibility in regard to any such agreements, and the enforcement thereof shall be the responsibility of the parties to the agreement.

Keeneland will not permit a horse entered in the sale to go through the auction ring if Keeneland has actual knowledge that the horse has been sold privately prior to said auction.

Notice is hereby given to all participants at Keeneland Sales that Keeneland may record any or all portions of Keeneland's sales by video, audio or other means.

First

APPLICABLE LAW; LIMITATION OF WARRANTIES: As stated above, the horses included herein are offered for sale according to the laws of the State of Kentucky which shall be controlling and apply in all respects. In accordance with KRS 355.2-328 (4) and other applicable laws, the right to

1

Fifth

LIMITATION OF WARRANTIES: OTHER THAN THOSE LIMITED WARRANTIES EXPRESSLY STATED IN THESE CONDITIONS OF SALE, OR UNLESS OTHERWISE EXPRESSLY ANNOUNCED AT TIME OF SALE, THERE IS NO GUARANTEE OF ANY KIND, EXPRESS OR IMPLIED, AS TO THE SOUNDNESS, CONDITION, WIND OR OTHER QUALITY OF ANY HORSE SOLD IN THIS SALE. HOWEVER, all horses that are cribbers must be so announced at the time of sale. For all horses that (i) possess any deviation from the norm in the eyes, (ii) are a "wobbler" (defined as a horse

Eighteenth

INSPECTION (INCLUDING THE REPOSITORY) All purchasers shall inspect fully each horse that they may purchase. As provided in the Conditions of Sale and otherwise, purchasers are accepting any horse purchased with all defects except those conditions and defects specifically warranted by Keeneland's Conditions of Sale. Purchasers that fail or refuse to inspect for any reason, including a lack of opportunity for inspection, purchase the horse at their own

It shall be the sole responsibility of the purchaser to determine the sufficiency, quality and completeness of the available inspection; however, full inspection shall include a review of all Repository information for each horse.

Keeneland will **not** review the Repository information and makes no warranty or assurance of any kind concerning the authenticity, sufficiency, quality, completeness or accuracy of the Repository information, all of which shall be the responsibility of the consignor. Knowledge of the Repository information therefore shall not be imputed to Keeneland.

Purchasers will be charged with knowledge of any defect that is or should be revealed by a reasonable inspection, including any defect that is or should be revealed by a review of the repository information, with the exception of the

Familiarize yourself with the conditions of sale, especially the sections that address announcement of medical conditions.

to have a specific defect.

Conditions of sale vary in comprehensiveness among companies, so review each company's conditions before attending one of its sales. Barretts, for example, keeps its conditions of sale focused on transactions relating to the buyer. Keeneland's conditions of sale are broader, spelling out the sales company and consignor responsibili-

ties, in addition to buyer responsibilities, with detailed verbiage. This means that some provisions that are stated in a separate document, the consignor's contract, might be duplicated in the conditions of sale.

As a case in point, Keeneland's twelfth condition of sale concerns catalog announcements and states that the accuracy of all information on the catalog page(s) is the

THINGS TO KNOW

Bidding on a horse at auction can be a daunting proposition. But if you follow these tips, you'll be bidding like a pro in no time.

- Find a reputable bloodstock agent to help you through all the steps.
- Be approved for credit. If you don't have established credit by the time you buy a horse, you may be required to pay in full at the time of sale.
- Set a limit on what you can spend — and stick to it.
- Become acquainted with your local sales company and auction team. Introduce yourself to the bid spotters. You can even let them know which horses you are interested in bidding on.
- Keep in mind that the opening bid on a horse is about 20 percent of the amount the horse is expected to bring.
- You don't have to raise the bid by the amount suggested. It can be a smaller or larger amount.
- If you are confused about how much you bid or where the bidding stands, notify your bid spotter at once.
- Take a deep breath, try to relax, and let the bidding begin!

sole responsibility of the consignor. This condition further states that it is the consignor's duty to report any inaccuracies to Keeneland by a certain time frame prior to the horse going on the auction block, so that the company may make an appropriate announcement before that horse's sale. By contrast, Barretts notes in its conditions of sale that catalog accuracy is the consignor's responsibility; however, Barretts covers this provision and other consignor responsibilities in greater detail in its consignor's contract.

Although there will be slight variations in the particulars regarding limited warranties, in general, horses are sold "as is" at a public auction, but certain physical conditions must either be announced when the horse goes into the ring or disclosed by veterinary certificate in the repository (see page 54). Failure to disclose the pertinent information (such as if the horse is a cribber, wobbler, ridgling, or twin; has an eye defect; or has had

invasive joint surgery, upper respiratory tract surgery, or abdominal surgery) can be grounds for rescinding a purchase, provided the purchaser notifies the sales company in writing within the prescribed right-to-return time frame set forth in the conditions of sale.

The time frame for returning a horse and the method used to resolve disputes related to physical condition vary according to the

ANNE M. EBERHARDT

The hip number.

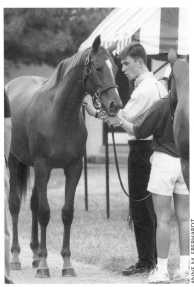

Inspecting a horse.

horse's physical condition and the sales company.

Buying and Selling Protocols

The auctioneer's patter booms over the public-address system. The pavilion's back walking ring is filled with prancing horseflesh heading to the auction ring. Coming toward you now is one of the horses you have chosen to bid on. Take a last look — and a deep breath. It's time to take your seat inside.

To be sure a bid spotter knows to look for you when the action starts, introduce yourself prior to the session during which you plan to bid. Eye contact is the key to communication between you and the bid spotter once the horse you want goes on the block.

Before raising your hand to bid, you and your adviser(s) will have performed countless permutations of a veritable Rubik's Cube of criteria for deciding which sale prospect(s) to try to buy. Ever hire

somebody from a long list of job applicants? Evaluating a catalog full of horses for your Thoroughbred operation is a similar process.

The sales catalog lists the horses being offered according to hip number, aptly named because after horses arrive on the grounds, a tag showing the assigned number is glued onto the horse's hips.

The catalog page provides pedigree information that, in fact, is a family resume. Is this broodmare a good producer, from a line of good producers? Is she in foal to a proven sire, or an exciting freshman (first-year) sire? What has this racing prospect's siblings or half siblings accomplished at the track? A hip is very hip indeed if that catalog page is laden with "black type" (boldface print denoting stakes wins or placings), and high dollar earnings.

Before you make the rounds of the barns to inspect prospects, check to see what horses have been

Attractive signage makes consignments easy to find.

scratched from the sale. Not every horse intended for auction makes it to the sales arena. Illness, private sale, and other factors can cause the withdrawal of a horse. Most sales companies post "outs" in strategic locations and also announce them before the start of individual sessions.

Your first visit to the barn to see how a prospect presents itself in the flesh is the initial screening interview. Bring a realistic sense of how much you are willing to pay; the obviously qualified candidates generally command higher bids. A second approving look from the buying team generally merits a veterinarian's review of the horse's health records. In this manner you whittle your bloodstock choices down to a short list, based on factors such as conformation (physical build), athleticism (how a racing prospect moves), and, yes, even a young animal's "professionalism," or composure and tempera-

Notes made while inspecting a horse.

ment under all of the pre-purchase scrutiny.

To give all buyers a chance to inspect their horses, consignors customarily ship horses to the sales grounds at least 24 to 48 hours prior to when the horse is due to sell. Particularly for a select sale, consignors like to have their horses on the grounds as many days before their sale date as the sales

Buyers watch a horse walk "down and back" during an inspection.

49

The Greatest Game

For newcomers to the Thoroughbred industry, selecting a bloodstock agent can seem as daunting as selecting a racing prospect. Unlike most professions, bloodstock agents do not have to have a license to conduct business. Yet, this is the person you are authorizing to advise and represent you.

In the interest of attracting and retaining new investors in Thoroughbred ownership, the National Thoroughbred Racing Association (NTRA), Thoroughbred Owners and Breeders Association (TOBA), Keeneland Association, and *The Blood-Horse* magazine have partnered to create "The Greatest Game, Inc." In 2003 The Greatest Game launched its consultant program, which matches new buyers with consultants — i.e., agents — who have been "vetted out" by The Greatest Game committee. The approved consultants, in joining the program, agree to adhere to a code of ethics that encompasses key issues such as principal's control and consent, commissions and fees, disclosure of conflicts of interest, and the all important competent representation, which requires the agent to have a substantial knowledge of the Thoroughbred industry, its customs, and its trade practices.

For more on The Greatest Game, contact TOBA at (859) 276-2291 or visit www.thegreatestgame.com.

company will allow. Inspecting a large number of horses while a big sale is underway can be hectic for consignors as well as for prospective buyers. Particularly when looking for racing prospects, many bloodstock agents get a head start on the catalog in the weeks before the sale by visiting the farms where young athletes are being prepped, to get their first looks at sale candidates.

Many of the larger breeding farms have a sales prep division. Others specialize in prep work, which entails overseeing the horse's diet, fitness, and grooming program, and schooling the horse to show well at the sale. Prep facilities will gladly schedule showings for interested buyers.

Transportation to the grounds, by horse van or trailer, is arranged by the consignor, or, in some cases, the seller if the horse was not boarded at the consignor's farm prior to the sale.

Sellers, by the way, can either represent themselves as the consignor when selling at auction, or enlist a third party or agent to serve as the consignor. An entire segment of the Thoroughbred industry consists of consignment operations that sell horses for other parties. However, even when selling through a consignor, the seller must list his name first on the sale entry form.

An entry form must be filed with the company for each horse that will be sold. To sell at auction, a horse must be entered in a sale by the deadline set by the sales company. There is also a deadline for when horses can be withdrawn from a sale, without owing the sales company its entry fee.

KEENELAND
Acknowledgement of Purchase and Security Agreement

Date _____ Sale Date _____

Hip Number _____ Purchase Price _____

Please print the following information:

Purchaser or Agent Name

Address

City, State, Zip Code, Country

Telephone

The purchaser hereby purchases and promises to pay the Keeneland Association the purchase price set forth for the horse described herein plus Kentucky sales tax at the rate of 6 % of the purchase price unless exempt under KRS 139.531 (2) (a) and (2) (b) (see below). **This purchase and payment therefore is made in accordance with the additional terms and conditions set forth on the back hereof and incorporated by reference herein.** In order to secure payment of the purchase price and all other expenses incurred by Keeneland, the purchaser hereby grants Keeneland Association, its successors and assigns, a security interest in and to the above described horse, and any other horses purchased, and any proceeds, progeny, and/or products thereof.

Purchaser acknowledges that he is familiar with the "Conditions of Sale" as printed in the catalogue and **the confirmation of purchase is subject to those conditions, the same being made a part hereof and incorporated by reference herein.**

OTHER THAN THOSE LIMITED WARRANTIES EXPRESSLY STATED IN THE CONDITIONS OF SALE, THERE ARE NO WARRANTIES, EXPRESS OR IMPLIED, BY SECURED PARTY OR CONSIGNOR AS TO MERCHANTABILITY OR FITNESS FOR ANY PARTICULAR PURPOSE OF ANY ANIMAL SOLD AND ALL ANIMALS ARE SOLD "AS IS".

Purchaser claims exemption from Kentucky Sales Tax *(Initial One)*

1. _____ The purchase is made for breeding purposes only; or
2. _____ The purchase is made by a non-resident of Kentucky of a horse less than two (2) years of age and will immediately be transported outside of Kentucky after the sale or following holding of the horse in Kentucky for training purposes; or
3. _____ The horse purchased is two years old or older, which is not sold for breeding purposes only, and will be immediately shipped by Keeneland Association, Inc., from Lexington, Kentucky to the purchaser at an out-of-state point via licensed Interstate Common Carrier (ICC). It is understood and agreed that such shipment shall be wholly at purchaser's risk. A release will be issued to ICC carrier upon receipt of bill of lading. All expenses incurred by Keeneland in shipping the horse will be invoiced to purchaser and Keeneland shall retain a lien in the horse to secure all such expenses.

<u>Notice:</u> The purchaser must make settlement with Keeneland for the full purchase price no later than thirty minutes from the fall of the hammer or have approved credit with Keeneland for this sale. The individual signing this agreement, regardless of the form of the signature or his signing capacity, agrees to be personally liable, jointly and severally with the purchaser, for the full purchase price if the purchaser does not make settlement within thirty minutes or have approved credit or if Keeneland has not been provided a signed buyer's authorized agent form granting purchase authority during this sale to the individual signing this agreement.

Rev. 9/00

Signature

Print Signature Name

Billing address if different than above

City, State, Zip Code, Country

Telephone

KEENELAND ASSOCIATION, INC., Secured Party

Example of a purchase agreement.

Some sales or sale sessions are designated as select, while others are open. Only horses that have been inspected and approved by the sales company's selection team are offered in a select sale or session. Select sale horses have met certain pedigree and conformation

Buyer's Authorized Agent

Date_____

To: **Keeneland Association, Inc.**   I have this day appointed

_____
(Print Name of Agent)

_____
(Address)

_____
(City, State, Zip)

_____
(Phone Number)   (Fax Number)

_____
(Email address)

to act for me for such period as indicated below. Said appointee, as my duly appointed and authorized agent, shall have full power and authority to act for me in any and all matters in connection with or arising out of the purchase of horses at Keeneland during the time period set forth herein. Said agent is further authorized to execute any and all documents in connections with the purchase(s) including granting **Keeneland Association, Inc.** a security interest in all horses purchased. I authorize said agent to do all things incidental to and in furtherance of the purchase of horses, and I agree to pay for all animals purchased by said agent on my behalf in accordance with Keeneland's Conditions of Sale. This agency is revocable only in writing.

> **The duration of agency shall be for this sale only unless otherwise indicated:**
>
> **through and including**   (date)_____.
> For purposes of this section, the term "sale" shall include any Internet RNA Sale which shall occur immediately after or during the sale.

Other Instruction _____

Signature _____

Print Name _____

Title (if applicable) _____

Address _____

_____

State of _____

County of _____

The foregoing instrument was acknowledged before me on the

_____day of_____, _____

by _____
                              (Name of Buyer)

as _____
                              (Title if Buyer is not individual)

for and on behalf of _____
                              (Firm Name if applicable)

My Commission expires _____

_____
Signature of Notary Public

Example of a buyer's authorized agent form.

criteria. For both select and open sessions, sales companies require an entry fee for each horse. At Keeneland the entry fee is $1,000, half due before the sale, and half due after.

Consignors make their consignments "buyer friendly" by outfitting their stalls and personnel in uniform colors and decking their area of the barn with plenty of signage. This makes the various consignments easy to identify as buyers navigate the grounds. Often, several small consignments are stabled in a single barn. Maps in the sales catalog help buyers locate barns and specific consignors.

When a prospective buyer arrives at a sales barn, a card person on the consignor's staff will hand the buyer a card that lists the hips offered. Those tags glued onto the horses' hips come in handy here. Buyers mark the card for the hips they want to see, and the grooms and showmen bring out each horse as the card person calls for it. Standard inspections begin with the showman standing the horse in a conformation pose, and then walking the horse "down and back" to the buyer. Prospective buyers make notes in their catalogs of what they like or dislike about a particular horse and whether it deserves a second look.

Now that you have your bloodstock selections narrowed down, you are ready to bid — or have your agent do the bidding.

Suppose you feel intimidated about bidding on a horse because it's your first time or you simply are not able to attend the sale in person. You can designate an agent to act as your representative to bid and sign the sales ticket for you by submitting the

TOM HALL

Signing a purchase agreement.

authorized agent form in the front of the catalog to the company's business office. (For help selecting a bloodstock agent, see Ch. 4, Auction Experts, and the sidebar on page 50 on The Greatest Game.) First-time buyers prepared to do their own bidding still should stop by the office first and have someone from the company walk them through the process — something the company will gladly do.

Suppose there is a dispute between two bidders as to who made the final bid? Or you intended to bid a different amount than what the auctioneer recognized? Notify a bid spotter immediately if you dispute a bid, before the sale ticket is signed. Resolution of bidding disputes is covered under the conditions of sale. If a dispute occurs, the auctioneer will adjudicate.

The right to bid is reserved for all sellers, including their disclosed and undisclosed agents. This means you might wind up bidding against the seller, and that brings us to the reserve.

Reserves

When you see a sales summary sheet and a horse is listed as "RNA," it stands for "reserve not attained," and it means the horse returned from the ring unsold. The

TOM HALL

Most consignors place a reserve on a horse before it sells.

reserve is the minimum price the consignor has decided a bidder will have to pay to take the horse home.

Setting a reserve is purely voluntary on the part of consignors, but if they choose to set one, and usually they do, consignors enter a reserve at the sales office's reserve counter by a certain time prior to when a horse is due to go into the ring. The reserve is never announced when the bidding begins — that would take all the fun out of the process. But in the heat of the moment, it pays to remember you might be the only "live" money bidding. You might be bidding against the seller, who is trying to attain a targeted price, or you might be bidding against the company, representing the seller, who has set a reserve.

Keep in mind that when consignors set a reserve, they are appraising the horse using their own evaluation system. It's up to you and your adviser(s) to appraise the horse as well. Set your prices going by your own budget, not based on the bidding. Decide when you want to be in, and when you want to be out, and stick to your limit.

If a horse fails to meet its reserve, a prospective buyer and the consignor often will work out a deal afterward in which the horse is sold privately.

Repository

Under the conditions of the major sales, it is the purchaser's responsibility to inspect the horse before it sells, and to review any veterinary certificates on file. As a service to buyers, the major sales companies have set up a repository, or information center, on their grounds. Here, your veterinarian can review radiographs (X-rays) and other veterinary records that consignors submit on the horses they are selling. This is a huge service to buyers. It allows them to conduct thorough pre-purchase inspections without running up a large bill obtaining numerous sets of radiographs and saves the buying team a bundle of time when a busy sale gets in full swing.

The advent of the repository means that those sellers who want to keep buyers coming back to their consignments are now picking up the tab for those complete sets of radiographs. Submitting radiographs and veterinary certificates to the repository is voluntary on the part of the seller. A complete set of radiographs consists of 32 standard views, as recommended by the American Association of Equine Practitioners. The going

rate veterinarians charge for a set of radiographs is from $500 to $700.

Sales companies require that any radiographs voluntarily submitted be taken within a certain time frame prior to the horse's sale date, generally within 15 to 21 days prior to the date the horse sells. This time frame will vary depending upon the sales company, and the specific sale. Video endoscopes of the upper respiratory tract or an endoscopic certificate also can be put on file in the repository, as well as veterinary statements pertaining to physical conditions that warrant disclosure.

ANNE M. EBERHARDT

Veterinarians review X-rays in the repository.

ANNE M. EBERHARDT

Buyers are responsible for arranging transport for newly purchased horses.

Veterinarians charge a fee to review information in the repository. The fee is based on how many horses' information the veterinarian evaluates for a buyer and will vary depending on the veterinarian involved and whether a physical examination of the horse(s) is included. A veterinarian might charge $75 to examine a horse in its stall, review repository information, and write a report on it.

The extent of the veterinary evaluation depends on how much information the buyer is seeking. Some veterinarians check acupuncture trigger points, look for any flaws such as asymmetrical limbs, listen to the heartbeat, and feel muscle tone. Veterinarians will charge a fee for any specific services, such as X-raying specific joints for about $10 to $15 per plate or performing an endoscopic exam at anywhere from $50 to $75 per scope.

Typically, a buyer gives a veteri-narian a short list. The list is culled based on endoscope exams that the buyer pays the veterinarian to perform. If the throat passes, the veterinarian will go look at the radiographs.

Protecting Yourself

One of the most important decisions you make is selection of an adviser (see chapter 4 on Auction Experts.) Finding someone you can trust and who has your best interests in mind is pivotal not only to your auction experience but your success as an owner.

Many an eager newcomer has fallen victim to unscrupulous characters sometimes acting on their own or in concert with sellers. Vet your advisers as closely as you would a prospective horse.

Sales move very quickly and occasional errors can occur. Be alert to the rhythm of an auction and the increments in which bids increase. If you think you bought a horse that the auctioneer knocks down to another party, alert your bid spotter. He or she may be able to reopen bidding.

Also, exercise some patience during bidding to ensure that you do not bid against yourself. And never bid on a horse you have not inspected, no matter how enticing the animal looks on the auction block.

Fall of the Hammer Coverage

Every couple of minutes at an auction, the hammer bangs down on the dais and ownership of the horse in the ring changes hands. In that instant, the consignor's equine mortality insurance ceases to cover the horse, and the buyer assumes the risk of ownership.

Fall of the hammer coverage takes effect immediately upon transfer of ownership, provided you have arranged for it beforehand. It is mortality insurance that covers you for loss of the purchase price in case of fatal injury, however soon it might occur after you acquire the horse.

If you plan to buy at auction, contact an equine insurance agent and provide the name that you or your representative will use to sign the ticket. Prospective buyers need not provide a hip number they'll be bidding on — most people planning to buy at public auction do not want to tip their hand. A blanket statement requesting fall of the hammer coverage is all that is required, and coverage will apply to any horses purchased at the sale.

It costs nothing to arrange for fall of the hammer coverage if you wind up not buying any horses. You pay for insurance only if you buy a horse.

The premium rate you pay will depend upon factors such as the age, purchase price, and use of the horse. For example, racehorses of either sex, ages two and up, carry the highest premium rate, at approximately 5.5 percent if purchased for up to $50,000, and approximately 5 percent if purchased for over that value. Weanling, yearlings, and breeding stallions typically would be insured at a 3.25 percent premium rate. Broodmares up to age 14 would be insured at 3.25 percent, but after age 14, the premium rate for broodmares increases with each year of age. The horse is insurable for the purchase price and no more.

Shipping

After buying at auction, you are responsible for transporting your new horse or horses off the sales grounds. Sales companies give buyers 24 to 48 hours to ship out their purchases, but most buyers attend to this detail more quickly than that. It simply makes sense for the welfare of the horse. Commercial van companies have agents at the sales and arrangements can be made with them. Or, if you find you are transporting horses regularly, you might invest in a private trailer. Sales company personnel will ask to see the stable release form issued by the sales office before letting the horse load.

Finally, be sure to notify the farm or training center where the horse is going to expect its arrival.

—*Bettina Cohen*

How to read a catalog page

A catalog page can seem confusing and intimidating at first glance. What do all those names and terms mean and how do you use them? But don't worry. Use these pointers to familiarize yourself with a horse's catalog page, and you will quickly learn to interpret the information to help you decide which horse you want. Examples of a yearling, two-year-old, and broodmare catalog page are included.

1 The number identifying the horse, appearing on its hip.

2 The horse's pedigree, traced three generations. At each generation the sire appears on the top and the dam on the bottom.

3 A synopsis of the sire's racing record and notable progeny.

4 A synopsis of the first dam's racing record and progeny.

5 The maternal grandmother.

6 A synopsis of the racing record of the second dam's most prominent offspring. Each indentation represents one generation.

7 The maternal great-grandmother.

8 Many states have special racing opportunities restricted to horses bred in their state. This will indicate if the horse is eligible for such a program.

9 A listing of upcoming stakes races to which the horse has been nominated.

10 Bold capital letters for a horse's name indicate the horse is a stakes winner. If its name appears in bold lower-case letters, the horse is stakes-placed.

11 The horse's birth date.

12 The horse's name. If unnamed, the horse is described by sex and color.

13 The name of the consignor (the farm or individual selling the horse).

14 Indicates the stakes race is graded and which grade.

YEARLING
Catalog Page

Hip No.
320

Consigned by
McMahon of Saratoga Thoroughbreds LLC, Agent

Chestnut Colt

		Forty Niner	Mr. Prospector
	Distorted Humor		File
		Danzig's Beauty	Danzig
Chestnut Colt			Sweetest Chant
April 20, 2000		Slewacide	Seattle Slew
	Belle's Good Cide		Evasive
	(1993)	Belle of Killarney	Little Current
			Cherished Moment

By DISTORTED HUMOR (1993), black type winner of 8 races, $769,964, Commonwealth Breeders' Cup S. [G2], Churchill Downs H. [G2]-ntr, Ack Ack H. [G3], Salvator Mile H. [G3], Screen King S., 2nd Fayette S. [G2], Jerome H. [G2], Kentucky Cup Classic H. [G3], 3rd Cigar Mile H. [G1], etc. His first foals are yearlings of 2001.

1st dam
BELLE'S GOOD CIDE, by Slewacide. 2 wins at 3, $26,696. This is her second foal. Her first foal is a 2-year-old of 2001, which has not started.

2nd dam
BELLE OF KILLARNEY, by Little Current. Unraced. Dam of 4 winners, including--
   BELLE OF COZZENE (f. by Cozzene). 9 wins, 3 to 5, $522,455, Arlington Matron H. [**G3**], Modesty H. [**G3**], Oaklawn Breeders' Cup H. [L] (OP, $94,350), Oklahoma Classics Day Distaff S. [R] (RP, $57,300), Sundance S. [L] (LS, $30,000), Oklahoma Classics Day Distaff S. [R] (RP, $28,350), 2nd Bel Air S. [R] (OP, $10,000), 3rd Three Chimneys Sprinter S. [**G1**], Lady Remington Breeders' Cup S. (RP, $5,425).
   QUACKERBELL (g. by Quack). 5 wins, 2 to 5, $111,918, Blue Ribbon Classic Laddie Futurity [L] (BRD, $43,353), Heritage Place Derby [R] (RP, $39,378), 2nd Blue Ribbon Classic Derby [R] (BRD, $6,987). Set ntr.

3rd dam
Cherished Moment, by Graustark. 4 wins at 2 and 3, $56,755, 2nd Ashland S.-**G3**. Dam of 6 winners, including--
   One Moment Please. 7 wins at 3 and 5, $99,898.
   Sunset Cloud. 2 wins at 3, $52,575. Producer.
   Summer Paradise. Unraced. Dam of 3 winners, including--
     GAYLA'S PLEASURE. 4 wins at 3, $79,212, Dixie Miss S. (LAD, $24,000), 3rd Coca-Cola Fair Grounds Oaks [**G3**]. Producer.

4th dam
PUMPKIN PATCH, by Bold Ruler. Unraced. Half-sister to **HAIL THE PIRATES** (sire), **CANDALITA** (dam of **OLYMPIC CIRCUIT**; granddam of **APPLE CURRENT** [**G3**]; etc.), **Full Curl**. Dam of 6 foals to race, all winners, including--
   Cherished Moment. Black type-placed winner, see above.
   Judge Mauck. 4 wins, 2 to 4, $46,876, 2nd Lakefront H. Sire.
   Precious Pumpkin. Winner at 3, $8,033. Dam of 5 winners, including--
     SHE'S ALWAYS RIGHT. 4 wins, 2 to 4, $69,763, Joan Alhadeff Lassies S. (YM, $31,185).
   Bunch of Smiles. Unraced. Producer. Granddam of **MIRACLE METS** (3 wins to 3, placed at 4, 2001, $44,080), **Proud Sunset** (4 wins, $100,405).

Breeders' Cup nominated.
Registered New York-bred.

5-01

Funny Cide's yearling catalog page.

1 The number identifying the horse, appearing on its hip.

2 The horse's pedigree, traced three generations. At each generation the sire appears on the top and the dam on the bottom.

3 A synopsis of the sire's racing record and notable progeny.

4 A synopsis of the first dam's racing record and progeny. In this case the subject horse is the mare's first foal, indicated after the mare's racing record.

5 The maternal grandmother.

6 The maternal great-grandmother.

7 A synopsis of the racing record of the third dam's most prominent offspring. Each indentation represents one generation.

8 Many states have special racing opportunities restricted to horses bred in their state. This will indicate if the horse is eligible for such a program.

9 A listing of upcoming stakes races to which the horse has been nominated.

10 Bold capital letters for a horse's name indicate the horse is a stakes winner. If its name appears in bold lower-case letters, the horse is stakes-placed.

11 The horse's birth date.

12 The horse's name. If unnamed, the horse is described by sex and color.

13 The name of the consignor (the farm or individual selling the horse).

14 The barn number where the consignor is located.

15 The maternal great-great-grandmother. When a catalog page goes back to the fourth dam, it is usually because the subject horse's dam is young with few offspring (such as in this case) or the female family or line is weak, with little or no black type in the first three generations.

16 The [L] indicates a listed or non-graded stakes. An [R] after a stakes name indicates the race is restricted, usually to horses bred in a particular state.

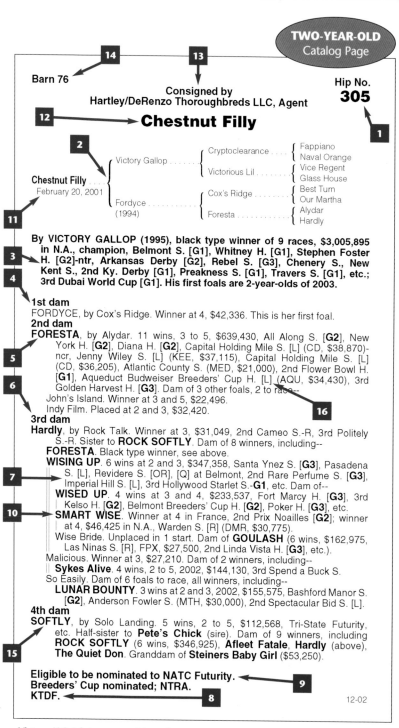

Barn 76

Consigned by
Hartley/DeRenzo Thoroughbreds LLC, Agent

Hip No.
305

Chestnut Filly

Chestnut Filly
February 20, 2001

```
                        ┌ Cryptoclearance ....  ┌ Fappiano
          Victory Gallop ┤                       └ Naval Orange
                        │                       ┌ Vice Regent
                        └ Victorious Lil ......  └ Glass House
                        ┌ Cox's Ridge .......   ┌ Best Turn
          Fordyce ......┤                       └ Our Martha
          (1994)        │                       ┌ Alydar
                        └ Foresta ...........   └ Hardly
```

By **VICTORY GALLOP** (1995), black type winner of 9 races, $3,005,895
in N.A., champion, Belmont S. **[G1]**, Whitney H. **[G1]**, Stephen Foster
H. **[G2]**-ntr, Arkansas Derby **[G2]**, Rebel S. **[G3]**, Chenery S., New
Kent S., 2nd Ky. Derby **[G1]**, Preakness S. **[G1]**, Travers S. **[G1]**, etc.;
3rd Dubai World Cup **[G1]**. His first foals are 2-year-olds of 2003.

1st dam
FORDYCE, by Cox's Ridge. Winner at 4, $42,336. This is her first foal.
2nd dam
FORESTA, by Alydar. 11 wins, 3 to 5, $639,430, All Along S. **[G2]**, New
York H. **[G2]**, Diana H. **[G2]**, Capital Holding Mile S. [L] (CD, $38,870)-
ncr, Jenny Wiley S. [L] (KEE, $37,115), Capital Holding Mile S. [L]
(CD, $36,205), Atlantic County S. (MED, $21,000), 2nd Flower Bowl H.
[G1], Aqueduct Budweiser Breeders' Cup H. [L] (AQU, $34,430), 3rd
Golden Harvest H. **[G3]**. Dam of 3 other foals, 2 to race--
John's Island. Winner at 3 and 5, $22,496.
Indy Film. Placed at 2 and 3, $32,420.
3rd dam
Hardly, by Rock Talk. Winner at 3, $31,049, 2nd Cameo S.-R, 3rd Politely
S.-R. Sister to **ROCK SOFTLY**. Dam of 8 winners, including--
FORESTA. Black type winner, see above.
WISING UP. 6 wins at 2 and 3, $347,358, Santa Ynez S. **[G3]**, Pasadena
S. [L], Revidere S. [OR], [Q] at Belmont, 2nd Rare Perfume S. **[G3]**,
Imperial Hill S. [L], 3rd Hollywood Starlet S.-G1, etc. Dam of--
WISED UP. 4 wins at 3 and 4, $233,537, Fort Marcy H. **[G3]**, 3rd
Kelso H. **[G2]**, Belmont Breeders' Cup H. **[G2]**, Poker H. **[G3]**, etc.
SMART WISE. Winner at 4 in France, 2nd Prix Noailles **[G2]**; winner
at 4, $46,425 in N.A., Warden S. [R] (DMR, $30,775).
Wise Bride. Unplaced in 1 start. Dam of **GOULASH** (6 wins, $162,975,
Las Ninas S. [R], FPX, $27,500, 2nd Linda Vista H. **[G3]**, etc.).
Malicious. Winner at 3, $27,210. Dam of 2 winners, including--
Sykes Alive. 4 wins, 2 to 5, 2002, $144,130, 3rd Spend a Buck S.
So Easily. Dam of 6 foals to race, all winners, including--
LUNAR BOUNTY. 3 wins at 2 and 3, 2002, $155,575, Bashford Manor S.
[G2], Anderson Fowler S. (MTH, $30,000), 2nd Spectacular Bid S. [L].
4th dam
SOFTLY, by Solo Landing. 5 wins, 2 to 5, $112,568, Tri-State Futurity,
etc. Half-sister to **Pete's Chick** (sire). Dam of 9 winners, including
ROCK SOFTLY (6 wins, $346,925), **Afleet Fatale**, **Hardly** (above),
The Quiet Don. Granddam of **Steiners Baby Girl** ($53,250).

Eligible to be nominated to NATC Futurity.
Breeders' Cup nominated; NTRA.
KTDF.

12-02

Victory U.S.A.'s two-year-old catalog page.

1 The number identifying the horse, appearing on its hip.

2 The horse's pedigree, traced three generations. At each generation the sire appears on the top and the dam on the bottom.

3 A synopsis of the sire's racing record and notable progeny.

4 A synopsis of the first dam's racing record and progeny.

5 The subject mare's race record.

6 The subject mare's produce record, shown by year foaled.

7 The produce record also shows years in which the subject mare did not deliver a foal and gives the reason as reported by the mare owner to The Jockey Club.

8 The name of the stallion to whom the subject mare has been bred and the date of the last mating.

9 Indicates whether the subject mare, based on recent veterinary examination, is thought to be in foal to the stallion listed as "mated to."

10 Bold capital letters for a horse's name indicate the horse is a stakes winner. If its name appears in bold lower-case letters, the horse is stakes-placed.

11 The horse's birth date, or in this case, the year foaled.

12 The horse's name. If unnamed, the horse is described by sex and color.

13 The name of the consignor (the farm or individual selling the horse).

14 The barn number where the consignor is located.

BROODMARE
Catalog Page

14 Barn
3 & 4

13 Consigned by Lane's End, Agent

12 **ISLAND JAMBOREE**
Bay Mare; foaled 1986

11

Hip No.
342

1

ISLAND JAMBOREE

2 ⟶

Exploudent ....
  Nearctic.......................
    ┌ Nearco
    └ *Lady Angela
  Venomous.......................
    ┌ Mel Hash
    └ Spiteful Sue

Careless Virgin ....
(1981)
  Wing Out ....
    ┌ Boldnesian
    └ Toulousette
  Careless Notion ....
    ┌ Jester
    └ Miss Uppity

3 **By EXPLODENT** (1969). Stakes winner of $101,421, Prince George's S., etc. Sire of 22 crops of racing age, 770 foals, 625 starters, 62 stakes winners, 481 winners of 2241 races and earning $32,056,111/$5,203(CAN) in N.A./U.S. Sire of dams of 56 stakes winners, including champions Fiji (GB), Crimson Quest, Warm Spell, Receton, and of Swearingen, Zoonaqua, Pulverizing, Linear, Valor Lady, Smiling and Dancin, Flanders, Sweet Baby James, Our Gatsby, Milt's Overture, Premier Explosion, Type Ryder.

4 **1st dam**

CARELESS VIRGIN, by Wing Out. Placed at 3 and 4, $8,745. Half-sister to **FABULOUS NOTION**, **CACOETHES [G1]**, **MARGARET BOOTH** [LR]. Dam of 9 registered foals, 9 of racing age, 9 to race, 6 winners, including **ISLAND JAMBOREE** (f. by Explodent, see record), **So Surprised** (f. by Eternal Prince, $54,112, 2nd Just Smashing S. (MED, $7,000)).

5 RACE RECORD: At 2, two wins, twice 2nd (Lady Luck S. (LAD, $7,000)); at 3, five wins (Lyrique H. [L] (LAD, $30,000), Chapel Belle S. (LAD, $21,000), Southland S. (LAD, $21,000), Senorita S. (LAD, $18,000), twice 2nd (Lorelei S. (LAD, $7,000)) in 10 starts; at 4, one win, 4 times 2nd (Louis R. Rowan H. [L] (SA, $20,000), Sangue H. [L] (LAD, $10,000)), once 3rd **6** (Dahlia H. **[G2]**); at 5, two wins (Run for the Roses S.-R (SA, $37,100)), 3 times 2nd (Gamely H. **[G1]**, Louis R. Rowan H. [L] (SA, $15,000)); at 6, unplaced in 1 start. Totals: 10 wins, 11 times 2nd, once 3rd. Earned $327,270.

PRODUCE RECORD:

1993 Emporium (GB), f. by Easy Goer. Unplaced in 2 starts. Producer.

1994 **FIJI (GB)**, f. by Rainbow Quest. 2 wins in 2 starts to 3 in England, Golden Daffodil S.; 6 wins in 10 starts at 4, $871,410, in N.A./U.S., champion **10** grass mare, Yellow Ribbon S. **[G1]**, Gamely Breeders' Cup H. **[G1]**, Santa Barbara H. **[G2]**, Santa Ana H. **[G2]**, 3rd Ramona H. **[G1]**, Vinery First Lady S. [L] (KEE, $55,850).

1995 **CAPRI**, c. by Generous. 3 wins at 3 in England, Gardner Merchant Cumberland Lodge S. **[G3]**, 2nd Barry Case Plant Hire John Porter S. **[G3]**, Bahrain Trophy, 3rd Queen's Vase **[G3]**; winner at 4 in France, Grand Prix de Chantilly **[G2]**.

1996 aborted single foal; 1997 unnamed c. by Darshaan, died at 2.

1998 Barbuda (GB), f. by Rainbow Quest. Unraced.

7 1999 Java (GB), f. by Rainbow Quest. Placed in 2 starts at 3 in England; winner at 3 and 4, 2003, $71,520, in N.A./U.S.

2000 not pregnant.

2001 Sigatoka, f. by Storm Cat. Unraced.

2002 c. by Kingmambo; 2003 not pregnant.

Mated to Point Given (Thunder Gulch--Turko's Turn), last service February 15, **8** 2003. (Believed to be **PREGNANT**).

KEE 11/03

9

63

How to read an Auction Edge® page

The more information you have as a buyer, the more able you are to make sound, scientific decisions. The catalog page is, of course, the place to start, but many things you need to know in order to place a value on a prospective purchase are not on a catalog page.

Auction Edge, published by Blood-Horse Publications, provides the additional data you need to help determine which horses to purchase. It complements the sales catalog by providing key data, such as stud fees, sales records of siblings, Beyer Speed Figures and Timeform ratings, and more.

1 Hip number is followed by sex, pedigree line, and breeder, and printed white on black to separate hips easily.

2 Tells when the first foals of the sire of the subject horse hit the ground. Following is the current-year stud fee of the sire and the stud fee that corresponds to the subject horse.

3 Family information gives number of starts, wins, and earnings for mares and foals and also shows previous sales.

4 Asterisks indicate exported horses.

5 Abbreviated non-productive year produce line.

6 Previous and current-year sales information of the subject horse's sire.

7 Last claiming price of mares and foals reflecting year, track, amount, and new owner.

8 Mare's and foals' Best Beyer® Speed Figure is shown, in addition to the best win, value of race, type of race, and track where he/she won (in the case of graded races, no dollar amount is given).

9 Hip number range at bottom of page allows for ease in locating desired horse.

1431 • Yrlg. c, by French Deputy—High Schemes, by High Echelon. Breeder Elk Manor Farm (Pa.)

First Foals: 1997; **2000 Stud Fee**: $17,500; **1998 Stud Fee**: $17,500   **Dosage**: (7-4-4-3-0) • **DI**: 2.60 • **CD**: 0.83
1999 Yrlg. Avg: $81,393 (42 **offered**, 28 **sold**) $67,500 **median**, $375,000 **high**, $2,000 **low**
2000 2YO Avg: $140,267 (18 **offered**, 15 **sold**) $135,000 **median**, $430,000 **high**, $2,500 **low**

Family	Best Win/Track	Beyer Rating
HIGH SCHEMES, 22 sts, 6 wins, $388,390	(gr. I)/Bel	97

    81KEESEP $9,500—Buyer, Joseph Morrissey
97—Con, c., by Polish Numbers. 9 sts, 1 win (D), $22,700 .... $26k/msw/PIM 76
    98FTKJUL $65,000—Buyer, Dogwood Stable
96—Lunar Eclipse, c., by Colonial Affair. Unraced .... n/a .... n/a
    97KEESEP $1,500—Buyer, Mary Laura White Stables
95-99—Marquee Chief, c., by Chief's Crown. 2 sts, 0 wins, $1,380 .... n/a .... n/a
    96KEESEP $23,000—Buyer, Golden State Stables
93—*Eishin Newton, c., by Seattle Slew. 14 sts, 0 wins, $36,106 .... n/a .... Jpn
    95KEEAPR $210,000—Buyer, Silky Green • **94KEESEP $40,000**—Buyer, John D. Gunther
91—Seattle Pioneer, c., by Slew o' Gold. 12 sts, 1 win (D), $13,590 .... $14k/msw/HIA 66
    92KEESEP $125,000—Buyer, Ikbal Khalil
90-95—Shared Prospect, c., by Mr. Prospector. 13 sts, 2 wins (D), $55,570 .... $26k/alw/BM 77
    91KEEJUL ($175,000) RNA • **94CLAIM (GG) $60,000;** For: J. A. Bolson
89—Lyphard's Shemes, c., by Manila. 4 sts, 0 wins, $103 .... n/a .... n/a
    92CALAUG $7,000—Buyer, Richard Tam • **90FTSAUG $150,000**—Buyer, Lonimar Stables
88—*Vermont*, c., by Chief's Crown. 27 sts, 7 wins (D), $199,085 .... $34k/alw/AQU 101
    89FTSAUG $450,000—Buyer, D. Wayne Lukas
87—*Range Glider, g., by Cox's Ridge. 6 sts, 2 wins (D), $3,667 .... n/a .... Mex
    91EPTAPR $2,200—Buyer, Espectaculos Y Deportes • **88FTSAUG $310,000**—Buyer, Mint Tree Stable
(**98**—Barren. **94**—Not bred. **92**—Foal died.)
Nicking: Sons of Deputy Minister/High Echelon mares: 5 foals, 4 strs, 3 wnrs (60%), 1 2yo wnr (20%), 1 SW (20%), 0 GSWs
          Sons of Deputy Minister/Native Charger mares: 3 foals, 2 strs, 2 wnrs (67%), 1 2yo wnr (33%), 1 SW (33%), 1 GSW (33%): **MILLIONS** (gr. III)

1432 • Yrlg. f, by Quiet American—How About Becky, by Broad Brush.
Breeder Dr. and Mrs. Thomas Bowman and Milton P. Higgins III (Md.)

    99KEENOV $55,000—Buyer, W.S. Overton, agent
First Foals: 1993; **2000 Stud Fee**: $35,000; **1998 Stud Fee**: $20,000   **Dosage**: (6-17-13-0-0) • **DI**: 4.54 • **CD**: 0.81
1999 Yrlg. Avg: $112,395 (26 **offered**, 21 **sold**) $67,000 **median**, $500,000 **high**, $3,300 **low**
2000 2YO Avg: $119,000 (5 **offered**, 3 **sold**) $42,000 **median**, $300,000 **high**, $15,000 **low**

Family	Best Win/Track	Beyer Rating
HOW ABOUT BECKY, 7 sts, 3 wins, $50,615	$40k stk/TIM	110

98—Expedia, f., by Polish Numbers. Unraced .... n/a .... n/a
97—How to Fly, f., by Fly So Free. Unraced
    97EASDEC $69,000—Buyer, Daniel Lopez
96—How 'bout Chris, f., by Unbridled. 2 sts, 0 wins, $500 .... n/a .... n/a
Nicking: QUIET AMERICAN w/BROAD BRUSH mares: 2 foals, 0 strs
          Sons of Fappiano/Broad Brush mares: 10 foals, 3 strs, 1 wnr (10%), 0 2yo wnrs, 0 SWs
          Sons of Fappiano/Ack Ack mares: 16 foals, 9 strs, 7 wnrs (44%), 1 2yo wnr (6%), 1 SW (6%), 1 GSW (6%): **CRYPTIC RASCAL** (gr. III)

1433 • Yrlg. c, by Atticus—Icy Folly, by Icecapade. Breeder Ellen B. Kill Kelley (Ky.)

First Foals: 1999; **2000 Stud Fee**: $20,000; **1998 Stud Fee**: $20,000   **Dosage**: (8-5-23-0-0) • **DI**: 2.13 • **CD**: 0.58

Family	Best Win/Track	Beyer Rating
ICY FOLLY, 25 sts, 4 wins,$244,478.	$50k stk/CD	105

    98KEENOV $75,000—Buyer, Ellen B. Kelley; {Atticus} • **94KEENOV $175,000**—Buyer, Three Chimneys Farm {Gone West}
    • **89KEENOV $450,000**—Buyer, Dan J. Agnew • **88KEESEP $300,000**—Buyer, D. Wayne Lukas
98—*San Sebastian*, c., by Miesque's Son. 5 sts, 1 win (T), $34,300 .... $24k/msw/MED 80
    99KEESEP $26,000—Buyer, John and Elizabeth Hamilton • **98KEENOV ($47,000)** RNA
97—*Pamambo, c., by Kingmambo. 9 sts, 2 wins (D), $0 .... n/a .... Pan
    98KEESEP $6,000—Buyer, Alberto Paredes
96—Zienat, f., by Woodman. Unraced .... n/a .... n/a
    97KEESEP $260,000—Buyer, Shadwell Estate Co. • **97KEEJUL ($135,000)** RNA
95—Shrewd, c., by Gone West. 27 sts, 1 win (D), $39,455 .... $15k/mcl/BEL 59
    99FTNAUG $28,000—Buyer, Nicolena P. Barone • **96KEESEP $95,000**—Buyer, Mrs. M.J. Dance Jr. • **95KEENOV ($105,000)** RNA
93—*Gallinaccia*, f., by Hansel. 31 sts, 6 wins (D), $58,559 .... $6k/alw/RD 71
    97KEENOV ($55,000) RNA; {Technology} • **95KEEAPR $21,000**—Buyer, Alex A. Moretti • **94KEESEP ($25,000)** RNA

A Buyer's Checklist

Before Arriving at the Sale, Did You...?

- Decide what kind of horse you would like to buy? e.g., colts, fillies, yearlings, two-year-olds, bays, chestnuts, sons/daughters of Storm Cat...
- Decide how much you can afford to spend?
- Obtain a sales catalog from the sales company?
- Familiarize yourself with the sales company's conditions of sale?
- Find an adviser or bloodstock agent to help you through the process?
- Apply and be approved for credit with the sales company?
- Reserve a seat in the bidding ring, if necessary?
- Contact an equine insurance agent about fall of the hammer coverage?

Don't Leave Home Without:

- Your sales catalog!
- Good walking shoes and comfortable clothes.

- Sunscreen (for those summer sales).
- Your favorite pen. Some consignors give them away, so you can get extras.
- Knowing how much you can spend!

At the Sale:

- Examine horses with your adviser and develop a "short list." Check for any catalog updates.
- Have a veterinarian "scope" your top choices and review their radiographs in the repository.
- Get to know the consignors you might buy from.
- Introduce yourself to the bid spotter for your bidding area.
- Plan your bidding strategy.
- Designate your adviser as your agent to bid if you don't want to do the bidding yourself.
- Notify a bid spotter immediately if you are disputing a bid.
- Arrange for transport for any horses you bought.

Buying a horse doesn't have to be an intimidating process.

BARBARA D. LIVINGSTON

4

Auction Experts

As one of the Thoroughbred industry's new investors, you may acquire a quick sense of familiarity with this otherwise complex business. You'll discover in no time what makes a strong catalog page, why stakes winners in a horse's family are so important, and how you can read and understand valuable stallion statistics.

"That is the beauty of this business; people quickly formulate their own opinions regardless of their experience," said Fred Seitz, owner of Brookdale Farm near Versailles, Kentucky. "Oddly enough, most people want to do it themselves either in whole or in part, and you see them go off in all kinds of different directions. Often unprepared, I think."

Seitz knows this because most of the people who contact him hoping to draw upon his nearly thirty years of experience as a farm owner, breeder, and sales consignor have already been in the business for several years.

"They realize they lack the experience and have made some mistakes and want to do better at what they are doing," he said.

The key is for you to get help, and lots of it, say Seitz and other industry experts. Your mantra should be simply: Don't go it alone.

The experts who can help the most generally fall into four categories: advisers/consultants, bloodstock agents, veterinarians, and trainers. You don't necessarily need to hire one of each. It depends on what you want to do with the horses you intend to buy. If you are considering pinhooking, buying a horse with the intention of reselling it at a profit, then you may never need a trainer. If you want to buy horses to race, then your trainer will probably want some say in what winds up in his barn. There is some crossover among the four categories. For example, an adviser may also be a bloodstock agent or a trainer. If an expert is wearing several hats, however, then a new owner needs to know without uncertainty how that expert is primarily making a living. The expert's main vocation could bias the advice given.

THINGS TO KNOW

The Thoroughbred Owners and Breeders Association is a great starting point when seeking information on entering the horse racing business. Visit the web site at www.toba.org or call (859) 276-2291.

Regardless of the category, the experts you choose should be intelligent, honest, experienced, and eager to communicate. Equally important is compatibility. You will be spending a lot of time with these people, so you had better enjoy their company.

Advisers/Consultants

The most important person you will find is an adviser or mentor.

You must have someone who is looking out for your interests first, a trait that is not always the case for experts in the other three categories.

A good first step toward finding that trusted adviser, or any expert, would be a call to the Thoroughbred Owners and Breeders Association, based in Lexington, Kentucky. The national organization has readily available a slew of information for new investors. TOBA, as it is known, can also provide you with phone numbers and contacts for every major state Thoroughbred association. The organization also has a program specifically for new and prospective owners called The Greatest Game, which has a dedicated web site at www.thegreatestgame.com. Besides providing you with information about the industry, The Greatest Game will match you with a consultant. You'll get a list of three consultants, who must sign a Code of Ethics to participate. These consultant are selected by lottery. It is then up to you to contact and interview them. (For more information about The Greatest Game, see Ch. 3, page 50.)

Don't stop there, though. Your next step is to work the phones. Call the president or executive vice president of your state association and get the names of five more people he would recommend as advisers. If no one with the association can make recommendations, at least get the names of people who can offer credible referrals. Then call the major sales company or companies in your region and get five more names from each. If you live near a racetrack, call a couple of the leading trainers (racing secretaries can help you find them) and get five more names from them.

"Take time and get references from the best people available," Seitz said. "The people who have the money to enter this business would never hire an accountant, or an attorney, or a physician without

ANNE M. EBERHARDT

Attending the sale with your advisers is a great way to learn the ropes.

references, in my opinion. But many times it is done off-handed."

Advisers may be farm owners or simply individuals who are knowledgeable about conformation, pedigrees, and market trends, and whose sole job is to find good horses for their clients.

Richard Hancock, executive vice president for the Florida Thoroughbred Breeders and Owners Association, said he first finds out how much prospective owners intend to spend, then takes them to

> **THINGS TO KNOW**
>
> Finding the right adviser can be the difference between success and failure in the horse racing business. Just remember to do your homework and check those references — just as you would do when hiring any professional — and you'll be well on your way to buying that first horse.

visit four or five breeding farms that operate within that budget.

"I tell them they are better off to visit with someone who has had their roots in the industry for awhile," Hancock said. "It is all about relationships. You want to give them a choice, and you don't want to put them into the hands of a sales person who just wants to make his 10 percent."

Some advisers may work for a flat fee, some will get a percentage of a horse's purchase price, and some may become partners or agree to a percentage of any profits made when horses are sold. In any case, know up front and have clearly defined what is expected and how the expert will be compensated.

Bloodstock Agents

Bloodstock agents may make good advisers, but their primary business is to buy and sell horses.

"If you are new, you have to rely on some expertise," Hancock said. "But you can't take it personally if you go to someone who is in the business of selling shoes, and he wants to sell you a pair of shoes."

Make no mistake about it, bloodstock agents know their markets. They know all the players and will usually work hard to find a horse for you to buy and even harder trying to get every dollar possible for a horse you're trying to sell.

As buyers, bloodstock agents will discuss what type of horse you want to buy and what you can expect to pay. They will look through the horses offered and help create a short list of horses to consider. Then they'll bid on the horses you are interested in. Bloodstock agents as buyers typically charge about 5 percent of a horse's purchase price for their commission. In the United States a bloodstock agent who only buys horses is a very rare thing. In Europe it is more common because it is more the norm for owners to use an agent. So, know going in that the person you're selecting to buy horses more than likely also has horses to sell.

As sellers, bloodstock agents typically charge a fee for every day a horse is on the sales grounds to cover expenses such as feed, straw, grooms' salaries, etc. Agents also get an average commission of 5 percent on a horse's purchase price. If the horse has a reserve price, which is a minimum price a seller says he must get before he lets a horse sell, and the final bid does not exceed that price, then the bloodstock agent typically gets 2.5 percent of the last bid when the auctioneer's hammer falls.

Be wary of agents who claim

A bloodstock agent can help you go through the catalog and narrow your choices.

they can do it all. Most bloodstock agents say it is nearly impossible to buy and sell horses at the same time and do a good job at either.

Veterinarians

Demi O'Byrne, veterinarian and international agent for the powerful Irish-based Coolmore breeding and racing outfit, once said that before the proliferation of radiographs and throat examinations on sale horses, he would buy a group of horses of which a third would be good, a third mediocre, and a third trash. Now, he said, buyers jump through all these examination "hoops" and a third of the horses are good, a third are mediocre, and a third are trash. So, how important are veterinarians at auctions? Very important, said several consignors and buyers. If you are going to spend $100,000 on a horse, isn't it worth the average cost of $190 that a veterinarian will charge to determine if that horse

has any major problem with its joints, throat, or heart?

Like any of the other experts, good veterinarians can be found by gathering names from people you meet at a sale. Once you have your short list of potential veterinarians, then interview them. You need to know a few things about what you want to do beforehand, such as what kind of horses you want to buy and how much risk you're willing to assume with your purchases. If you want to buy yearlings, then you need a veterinarian with a lot of experience looking at young horses. Racetrack practitioners don't necessarily make the best evaluators of young horses, say some vets. A racetrack practitioner who has experience with both young horses and racehorses is ideal.

Also, you should not expect your veterinarian to say, "buy this one" or "don't buy that one," even though some vets will. Most veterinarians see themselves as educators and facilitators between buyers and sellers. They gather all the information requested on a horse, evaluate the data, and then present their findings to you so you can make the final decision.

"It is not our business to pass/fail horses," said one veterinarian. "Every buyer has a different risk level and a different purpose intended. The buyer has the long pants on. He's writing the checks. The owner is charged with the task of becoming educated, knowing their risk tolerance, and knowing what their goal is."

Trainers

The closer a sale prospect is in getting to the racetrack, the more likely a trainer will attend a sale to look at it. Trainers are a common sight at two-year-olds in training sales and are downright scarce at weanling sales. Several trainers will attend the better yearling sales around the country. Many trainers prefer to have certain people break and train the young horses that will end up in their stables. Breaking horses is an art in itself, and if done properly prevents the trainer from having to deal with behavioral and other problems down the road. Trainers usually have their own scouts that sort through the yearlings being offered in a sale and compile a short list to be reviewed when the trainers get into town. A trainer who already has

this arrangement is a big plus for you. It is asking a lot for one person to evaluate a sale that may have, as in the case of Keeneland's September yearling sale, more than 4,000 horses entered.

If you are interested in racing, know that a trainer's eye for horses can be invaluable in identifying the ones that may not have fashionable pedigrees but possess the right physical traits to be runners. After all, standing in the winner's circle is much more fun than buying the most expensive horse in a sale.

The Team

Once you've assembled your team, some experts say it is a good idea to spend several months at the

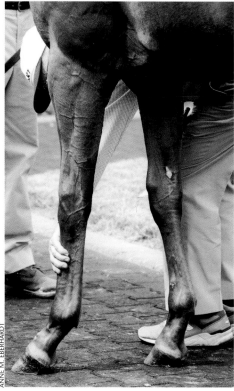

ANNE M. EBERHARDT

Trainers know what physical traits to look for in racehorses.

sales and "trade on paper" first. This way you can refine your goals and criteria before any real money is spent. Once you decide to start buying, you would do well to remind yourself periodically why you've assembled a team. You may see your key adviser stop bidding on a horse you or your spouse has fallen in love with because it has become too expensive or pass on another one because of some other problem. Don't get frustrated or impatient. The expertise is there, so remember to pay attention to the advice.

—*Eric Mitchell*

5

What Horses Cost

Imagine a hypothetical scenario in which you could sell the same horse at 10 different public auctions on 10 consecutive days. Could you expect the same price at each sale? No. In fact, getting the same price at any two would be a fluke.

How can that be? Why wouldn't the horse be worth the same on Monday as on Tuesday? Why wouldn't it sell for the same amount in California as it would in Kentucky?

Consider this. If you sold the same car at different auto auctions on subsequent days, would it bring the same price? Well, probably not.

A myriad of factors can determine the value of an object, and nowhere is that more true than inside a horse sale pavilion.

Some of the factors are the same whether you're selling a horse or an automobile. Foremost is the obvious: how many buyers are interested in your product? But with a

> ### THINGS TO KNOW
>
> Information on stud fees can be found in several locations including *The Blood-Horse Stallion Register* and *Auction Edge*, a supplemental guide to sales catalogs providing pertinent updated information on each sale horse. Also, *The Blood-Horse* has a thorough online stallion register: www.stallionregister.com.

horse auction, there are many more factors that are unique to its marketplace. What is the state of the economy and the stock market? What is the status of the guidelines affecting the tax treatment of horses? Are racetracks enjoying an increase or decrease in attendance and wagering? Are stud fees, the figure paid to have a broodmare mated to a stallion, up or down?

With horses, so many factors are at work: the pedigree, or parentage of the horse; conformation of the animal; market in which it is being sold; placement in the catalog; and circumstances under which it is being sold. Even the weather can be a factor.

Pedigree

The simple explanation of a pedigree is that it contains the names of a horse's ancestors. It is the horse's family tree. Of course, nothing is that simple. The names represent the genes that produced the animal and serve as a starting point for selecting horses at auction. Certain sires and sire lines are more desirable to some buyers. A buyer wanting a speedy juvenile may look for certain sires while a buyer desiring to race in Europe may seek out altogether different sires.

The pedigree also has much to say about what range a yearling might bring. If sire "A" has a stud fee of $100,000 and sire "B" has a stud fee of $2,500, it only stands to reason that sire "A" should have a higher average at auction for his progeny.

In addition to the stud fee, you should also consider the following factors:

• how many foal crops he has sired and the number of foals in each crop;

• the percentage of winners and stakes winners he has produced;

• his age.

A Kentucky Derby winner's first yearlings to sell at auction likely will generate more interest than that same horse's yearlings two years later unless he has had a slew of winning two-year-olds.

This is not to say only the sire line is important. The section of the pedigree relating to the dam's family and her produce is equally, if not more important. For instance, if a horse's dam has already shown she can produce quality runners, then buyers are

2003 Derby winner Funny Cide was a bargain yearling for $22,000.

more willing to purchase her latest offspring. Conversely, if a mare has produced five foals of racing age and none are winners of note, buyers will not be as interested in her young produce.

In addition to the mare's pro-

duce record, other considerations include:

• the produce records of her dam and granddam;

• the success or lack of success of the mare's full or half siblings.

As you become a more experienced buyer, you likely will become familiar with various breeding theories. Some of the better known include:

• Inbreeding, in which the same ancestor appears on both sides of the pedigree of a horse's first five generations;

• Outcrossing, in which none of the horse's ancestors appear more than once within the first five generations;

• Nicking, or the compatibility of certain bloodlines.

As a prospective buyer, you will find that horses that have won top races, called stakes races, are noted in the catalog by black type. Because of this catalog designation, stakes-winning horses are also referred to as black-type winners. Only the top few percent of races run each year — not just in the United States but other countries as well — are designated as stakes races and qualify for black-type status. As you study more catalog pages, you will be able to distinguish the difference between a black-type race worth $500,000 and one worth $50,000. You will also learn to distinguish good black-type families from those of lesser quality.

Typically, horses with the more select pedigrees are found at the "select" sales, such as those conducted in Kentucky by Keeneland and in Kentucky and other states by Fasig-Tipton. But this by no means implies regional auctions do not offer some attractive pedi-

ANNE M. EBERHARDT

2000 Derby winner Fusaichi Pegasus sold for $4 million as a yearling.

grees. More often than not, however, regional sales offer more reasonably priced horses...and there are reasons why. One of those reasons is the horses bred to the higher-priced stallions will mostly sell at "select" sales, leaving mostly lesser-pedigreed horses to sell elsewhere.

A person wanting to purchase $300,000 yearlings would probably not attend a sale that averages $10,000. *The Blood-Horse Auctions*, an annual supplement summarizing all sales, lists the pertinent information about each auction. For example, in August of 2003, a dozen different yearling sales were held with such varying averages as

Fasig-Tipton Saratoga (New York), $313,357; Ocala (Florida) Breeders Sales Co. open sessions, $9,539; and Fasig-Tipton Texas, $12,301.

Of course, value, whatever you define that as, can come at any level. Take these two examples:

At the 2001 Fasig-Tipton New York sale of preferred yearlings, P.A. "Tony" Everard paid $22,000 for a son of Distorted Humor. He later sold the horse, then gelded, privately. The bargain yearling was Funny Cide, winner of the 2003 Kentucky Derby and Preakness Stakes.

Japanese owner Fusao Sekiguchi paid $4 million at the 1998 Keeneland July yearling sale for a Mr. Prospector colt he named

THE BLOOD-HORSE

The great gelding John Henry brought a mere $1,100 as a yearling and went on to earn more than $6.5 million.

Fusaichi Pegasus. The colt won the 2000 Derby and later was sold by his owner for stud duties for a price reported in excess of $60 million.

Conformation

They say that beauty is in the eye of the beholder. That certainly holds true when horses are being evaluated for purchase. Often, simply by watching them stand and walk, prospective buyers will determine whether to spend thousands, hundreds of thousands, or millions of dollars.

Judging how a horse is put together physically is a very subjective process, akin to two people watching the same movie and walking away with very different opinions.

Two horses by the same sire and out of very similar mares will not bring the same price. In fact, two horses by the same sire and out of the same mare will likely not bring the same price. The reason, most likely, is a difference in conformation.

Suppose one trainer has instructions to find a horse that can sprint on the dirt, while another trainer has been told to search for a horse that can run long distances on the grass. They may look for not only different pedigrees but different types of conformation as well.

Do buyers purchase horses that have conformation flaws? The answer would be every day at every sale. The "perfect" horse has never been born, just like the perfect person. But that doesn't stop horsemen for searching for horses they think will become winners on the racetrack. The great champion John Henry, whose conformation left much to be desired, sold for $1,100 at auction and earned more than $6.5 million on the track.

However, horsemen seek certain desirable characteristics no matter what the price range. These characteristics include balance and good proportion, musculature, and bone mass. In initially assessing a horse, knowledgeable buyers also consid-

76

er whether the horse has "presence" and intelligence.

Although a horse should be judged as a whole rather than a collection of individual parts, it's important to scrutinize the components. Most horsemen will avoid:

• poor-quality feet and club feet;

• pasterns with too much or too little angle;

• horses that are over or back at the knees;

• pigeon toes or splay toes;

• a swayed back;

• hocks with too much or too little curve.

Experienced buyers always will watch a horse walk, looking at it from the side and front. Many conformation defects will manifest as a horse moves.

It requires looking at hundreds,

even thousands of horses to develop an eye for conformation. Even before you make your first bid, take the time to watch as many horses as you can, whether at the sales or in the paddock of a racetrack. Your dedication to developing an eye will pay dividends in the sales arena.

Marketplace

If you attend a "select" sale (those featuring horses the sale company has selected based on pedigree and conformation), you can expect to pay higher prices than at a regional "open" sale. Items sold at Sotheby's would be expected to bring more than those sold at Joe's Auction House. But both auction markets are necessary.

The majority of horses sold in Kentucky will bring more than

RACING SUCCESS OF $100,000-PLUS YEARLINGS

FTKJUL (Fasig-Tipton Kentucky July)   FTSAUG (Fasig-Tipton Saratoga)   KEESEP (Keeneland September)

SALE	$100K YEARLINGS	RNRS (% YRLGS)	WNRS (% YRLGS)	SW (% YRLGS)	GSW (% YRLGS)	G1SW (% YRLGS)
1999 $100,000+ YEARLINGS						
FTKJUL	70	63 (90%)	47 (67%)	9 (13%)	3 (4%)	0 (0%)
FTSAUG	130	111 (85%)	88 (68%)	11 (8%)	7 (5%)	3 (2.3%)
KEESEP	606	530 (87%)	416 (69%)	52 (9%)	28 (5%)	11 (1.8%)
1999 Totals	**1339**	**1162 (87%)**	**879 (66%)**	**121 (9%)**	**69 (5%)**	**26 (1.9%)**
2000 $100,000+ YEARLINGS						
FTKJUL	82	70 (85%)	51 (62%)	6 (7%)	4 (5%)	1 (1.2%)
FTSAUG	111	94 (85%)	69 (62%)	9 (8%)	6 (5%)	1 (0.9%)
KEESEP	681	547 (80%)	370 (54%)	35 (5%)	17 (2%)	5 (0.7%)
2000 Totals	**1431**	**1185 (83%)**	**796 (56%)**	**97 (7%)**	**53 (4%)**	**15 (1%)**
2001 $100,000+ YEARLINGS						
FTKJUL	85	62 (73%)	38 (45%)	5 (6%)	3 (4%)	1 (1.2%)
FTSAUG	150	106 (71%)	49 (33%)	6 (4%)	4 (3%)	1 (0.7%)
KEESEP	622	441 (71%)	216 (35%)	38 (6%)	21 (3%)	3 (0.5%)
2001 Totals	**1343**	**980 (73%)**	**475 (35%)**	**65 (5%)**	**37 (3%)**	**6 (0.4%)**
OVERALL RESULTS						
FTKJUL	237	195 (82%)	136 (57%)	20 (8%)	10 (4%)	2 (1%)
FTSAUG	391	311 (80%)	206 (53%)	26 (7%)	17 (4%)	5 (1%)
KEESEP	1909	1518 (80%)	1002 (52%)	125 (7%)	66 (3%)	19 (1%)
Overall Totals	**4113**	**3327 (81%)**	**2150 (52%)**	**283 (7%)**	**159 (4%)**	**47 (1.1%)**

ANNE M. EBERHARDT

Shop at sales that best fit your budget.

those sold in, say, Oregon. Buyers wishing to spend $100,000 for a yearling will attend different sales, or even different sessions of the same sale, from those wanting to spend $5,000. If you wish to spend $5,000, it makes no sense wasting time examining horses at an auction known to average $200,000.

Sale histories are easily accessed, and you would be wise to shop where you will have the best chance of finding, and purchasing, horses within your budget.

Each and every year, there are horses that are purchased for $10,000 that go on to win $500,000. But these are few and far between. More often than not, a horse brought $10,000 for a reason. You often hear, "he outran his pedigree," or "he was a diamond in the rough." Because they are horses, not widgets, this will always happen. But history shows horses purchased at "select"

sales have a higher percentage of winning more in purse money and becoming stakes winners.

Catalog

Horse sales can last many days. A Keeneland September or November sale may extend over two weeks. Traditionally, the horse perceived to be worth more sells on the first few days, and then the average decreases slightly on subsequent days.

But what about a one- or two-day sale?

Catalogs are generally arranged alphabetically by the first letter of the dam or broodmare's name. The starting letter is chosen blindly. Thus, if the letter "j" is chosen, that will be the starting point for each day, those beginning with "i" selling last. Sales company officials use their years of experience, aided by computer programs in recent years, to place horses in each day's catalog. Consignors also give useful input regarding what day their horses should be sold. It does not help how a consignor is perceived to have his horses selling for considerably less than the day's average.

For example, at the 2003 Keeneland September yearling sale, the horses sold on the first day of the auction averaged $365,788. Those sold on the final day (day 12) sold for an average of $7,798. Someone wanting to purchase $100,000 yearlings would not arrive in town for the auction's final few days.

Circumstances

Who is selling the horse and why?

Is the horse owned by a breeder that sells all of the horses he breeds every year? Is the horse owned by a

CLASSIC WINNERS PURCHASED AT AUCTION

YEAR WON	WINNER	CLASSIC RACE	SALE PRICE	SALE	YEAR SOLD
2003	Funny Cide	Kentucky Derby Preakness Stakes	$22,000	FT Saratoga	2001
2002	War Emblem	Kentucky Derby Preakness Stakes	$20,000	Keeneland Sept.	2000
	Sarava	Belmont Stakes	$190,000	FTMid. October	2000
			$250,000	FTF February	2001
2001	Monarchos	Kentucky Derby	$170,000	FTF February	2000
2000	Fusaichi Pegasus	Kentucky Derby	$4,000,000	Keeneland July	1998
	Commendable	Belmont Stakes	$575,000	Keeneland July	1998
1999	Lemon Drop Kid	Belmont Stakes	$200,000	Keeneland Sept.	1997
1998	Real Quiet	Kentucky Derby Preakness Stakes	$17,000	Keeneland Sept.	1996
	Victory Gallop	Belmont Stakes	$25,000	Keeneland Sept.	1996
1997	Silver Charm	Kentucky Derby Preakness Stakes	$16,500 $100,000	OBS August OBS April	1995 1996
	Touch Gold	Belmont Stakes	$180,000 $375,000	Keeneland Nov. Keeneland July	1994 1995
1996	Editor's Note	Belmont Stakes	$125,000	Keeneland Sept.	1994
1995	Thunder Gulch	Kentucky Derby Belmont Stakes	$40,000	Keeneland July	1993
	Timber Country	Preakness Stakes	$500,000	Keeneland July	1993
1994	Go for Gin	Kentucky Derby	$32,000 $150,000	FTK November FT Saratoga	1991 1992
1993	Colonial Affair	Belmont S.	$100,000	FT Saratoga	1991
1992	Lil E. Tee A.P. Indy	Kentucky Derby Belmont Stakes	$25,000 $2,900,000	OBS April Keeneland July	1991 1990
1991	Hansel	Preakness Stakes Belmont Stakes	$150,000	Keeneland Sept.	1989
1990	Unbridled Summer Squall	Kentucky Derby Preakness Stakes	$70,000 $300,000	Tartan-Nerud Keeneland July	1987 1988
1989	Sunday Silence	Kentucky Derby Preakness Stakes	$32,000	Cal March	1988
1988	Winning Colors Risen Star	Kentucky Derby Preakness Stakes	$575,000 $210,000 $300,000	Keeneland July Keeneland July FTF February	1986 1986 1987

Successful consignors can have an impact on sale prices.

breeder who often races horses? Is the horse being sold as part of a complete dispersal — the liquidation of a person's bloodstock holdings?

It is important for you to try and ascertain certain information about the horses upon which you are planning to bid. The consignor will have such information. This could include ownership information (whether partners are involved) and a health history.

When a broodmare sold in 2003 for $7.1 million, it was important to know that the buyer already owned half of her at the time she was auctioned. Thus, his expenditure was only half of the final hammer price.

Consignors at auction have the right to bid on their own horses and do so frequently. This is a way of "protecting" a horse's appraised value. Also, the person selling the horses may set a "reserve" price, a figure above which he will sell the horse in question. Reserve prices are not announced but are known to the auctioneer and his staff. A horse failing to reach its reserve price will be listed by the auction company as not sold, with the notation "reserve not attained (RNA)."

When horses are sold as part of dispersals, buyers are usually informed if the owners, or their representatives in the case of estate sales, will be bidding. These horses are often highly desirable as they have never been on the open market. It may not be the most pleasant sentiment, but it is often heard that "a dead man's horses sell well."

Odds and Ends

Many other factors can influence what happens at a horse sale. Here are just a few:

Weather: Many horsemen have noted that horses seem to sell better in bad weather. Perhaps this is only a perception. Or perhaps this is the reason — buyers think others may not make the sale in inclement weather; when they do, the prices are driven up.

Flow: The flow of a sale is very important. If prices are high at the start of a session, this momentum often times carries through the entire session. Adrenaline is not to be underestimated at auctions. At a long sale, say one lasting two weeks, the energy of a sale can carry over. For instance, if days one, two, and three are stronger than expected, then many buyers unable to fill their orders will ensure that subsequent sessions are stronger than expected, much like a domino effect.

Buyer Presence: A major buyer or two attending a sale, in addition to their regular agents or representa-

tives, can make a difference. People often bid more when present than when setting spending limits over the phone.

Sires: The death of a sire can certainly impact how his offspring sell. With buyers aware that there will be no more foals by a leading sire, they may be willing to pay more for the foals from his final few crops.

Success: A certain buyer's or consignor's success at recent sales certainly can impact a sale. If a consignor has been the leading consignor at a particular sale for 10 straight years, there must be a reason why. Also, if a purchaser has had luck buying from a particular consignor, he is more likely to consider the products from that seller.

Return on Investment: Does every buyer expect to recoup his return on investment with racetrack earnings? No. Many buyers take residual value into strong consideration when making purchases. If the colt runs well enough to become a stallion prospect, his value could escalate dramatically. If the filly is unable to run, what might she be worth as a broodmare?

As you see, many factors determine a horse's price. Deciding the level at which you want to play, then doing your homework can help take some of the guesswork out of buying at auction. It takes years of experience to become competent at placing a value on a horse. Even so, a horse is worth what the market will pay. All it takes is two interested parties.

—*Dan Liebman*

ALL-TIME TOP-SELLING YEARLING COLTS

PRICE	NAME	PEDIGREE	CONSIGNOR	BUYER	SALE	YEAR
$13,100,000	Seattle Dancer	Nijinsky II—My Charmer, by Poker	Warner L. Jones Jr.	BBA (England)	KeeJul	1985
$10,200,000	Snaafi Dancer	Northern Dancer—My Bupers, by Bupers	Crescent Farm	Aston Upthorpe Stud	KeeJul	1983
$8,200,000	Imperial Falcon	Northern Dancer—Ballade, by Herbager	Windfields Farm	BBA (England)	KeeJul	1984
$7,100,000	Jareer	Northern Dancer—Fabuleux Jane, by Le Fabuleux	Bruce Hundley, agt.	Darley Stud Management	KeeJul	1984
$7,000,000	Laa Etaab	Nijinsky II—Crimson Saint, by Crimson Satan	Tom Gentry	Gainsborough Farm	KeeJul	1985
$6,800,000	Tasmanian Tiger	Storm Cat—Hum Along, by Fappiano	Lane's End, agt.	Demi O'Byrne	KeeSep	2000
$6,500,000	Anjaad	Seattle Slew—Desiree, by Raise a Native	Spendthrift Farm, agt.	Darley Stud Management	KeeJul	1984
$6,400,000	Van Nistelrooy	Storm Cat—Halory, by Halo	Lane's End, agt.	Demi O'Byrne	KeeSep	2001

ALL-TIME TOP-SELLING YEARLING FILLIES

PRICE	NAME	PEDIGREE	CONSIGNOR	BUYER	SALE	YEAR
$4,400,000	Moon's Whisper	Storm Cat—East of the Moon, by Private Account	Lane's End, agt.	Shadwell Estate	KeeSep	2000
$4,000,000	Showlady	Theatrical (Ire)—Claxton's Slew, by Seattle Slew	Lane's End, agt.	John Ferguson Bloodstock	KeeSep	2000
$3,800,000	Illusive Serenity	Gone West—Touch of Greatness, by Hero's Honor	Three Chimneys Sales, agt.	John Ferguson Bloodstock	KeeSep	2003
$3,750,000	Alchaasibyeh	Seattle Slew—Fine Prospect, by Mr. Prospector	Spendthrift Farm	Darley Stud Management	KeeJul	1984
$3,700,000	Virtuosa	Seeking the Gold—Escena, by Strawberry Road (Aus)	Denali Stud, agt.	Reynolds Bell Jr., agent	KeeJul	2001
$3,600,000	Born Perfect	Mr. Prospector—Molly Girl, by Seattle Slew	Taylor Made Sales Agency, agt.	Padua Stables	KeeJul	2000
$3,400,000	Sophisticat	Storm Cat—Serena's Song, by Rahy	Denali Stud, agt.	Demi O'Byrne	KeeJul	2000
$3,400,000	Inkling	Seeking the Gold—Number, by Nijinsky II	Claiborne Farm	Demi O'Byrne	KeeJan	1998
$3,000,000	Ustoura	Storm Cat—Inca Legacy, by Saratoga Six	Gainesway, agt.	John Ferguson Bloodstock	KeeJul	2001
$2,800,000	Platinum Heights	Storm Cat—Amelia Bearhart, by Bold Hour	David and Ginger Mullins, agts.	Eugene Melnyk	KeeJul	2002
$2,800,000	Gone to the Moon	Gone West—Miraloma, by Deputy Minister	Denali Stud, agt.	Padua Stables	KeeJul	1999

PROGRESSION OF YEARLING SALE PRICES

YEAR	NAME	SEX	PEDIGREE	CONSIGNOR	BUYER	SALE	PRICE
1917	*Huron II	c	*Sweeper—Zuna, by Hamburg	no record	Joseph Widener	FTSAug	$4,000
1917	The Saint	c	*Sain—Nannette, by Yankee	no record	S.D. Riddle	FTSAug	$4,000
1918	Royal Jester	c	Black Jester—*Primula II, by St. Denis	no record	J.K.L. Ross	FTSAug	$14,500
1919	Sun Turret	c	Sunstar—*Marian Hood, by Martagon	P.M. Walker	J.K.L. Ross	FTSAug	$25,000
1925	War Feathers	f	Man o' War—*Tuscan Red, by William Rufus	Cary T. Grayson	James C. Brady	FTSAug	$50,500
1927	Hustle On	c	Hurry On—*Fatima II, by Radium	Himyar Stud	W.R. Coe	FTSAug	$70,000
1928	New Broom	c	Whisk Broom II—Payment, by *All Gold	Mrs. T.J. Regan	Eastland Farm	FTSAug	$75,000
1954	Nalur	c	*Nasrullah—Lurline B., by *Alibhai	Clifford Mooers	F.J. Adams	KeeJul	$86,000
1956	*Rise 'n Shine	c	*Hyperion—Deodara, by Dante	Newstead Farm	Mrs. M.E. Lunn	FTSAug	$87,000
1961	Swapson	c	Swaps—Obedient, by *Mahmoud	Spendthrift Farm	John M. Olin	KeeJul	$130,000
1964	One Bold Bid	c	Bold Ruler—Forgetmenow, by Menow	Warner L. Jones Jr.	Mrs. Velma Morrison	KeeJul	$170,000
1966	Bold Discovery	c	Bold Ruler—La Dauphine, by *Princequillo	Spendthrift Farm	Frank McMahon	KeeJul	$200,000
1967	Majestic Prince	c	Raise a Native—Gay Hostess, by *Royal Charger	Spendthrift Farm	Frank McMahon	KeeJul	$250,000
1968	Reine Enchanteur	f	*Sea-Bird II—*Libra, by *Hyperion	Mrs. Julian Rogers	W.P. Rosso	KeeJul	$405,000
1970	Crowned Prince	c	Raise a Native—Gay Hostess, by *Royal Charger	Spendthrift Farm	Frank McMahon	KeeJul	$510,000
1973	Wajima	c	Bold Ruler—*Iskra, by Le Haar	Claiborne Farm	J.A. Scully, agt.	KeeJul	$600,000
1974	Kentucky Gold	c	Raise a Native—Gold Digger, by Nashua	Spendthrift Farm	Mr. & Mrs. Wallace Gilroy	KeeJul	$625,000
1975	Elegant Prince	c	Raise a Native—Gay Hostess, by *Royal Charger	Spendthrift Farm	Mr. & Mrs. Franklin Groves	KeeJul	$715,000
1976	Canadian Bound	c	Secretariat—Charming Alibi, by Honeys Alibi	Bluegrass Farm	Blue Meadow Farms	KeeJul	$1,500,000
1979	Hoist the King	c	Hoist the Flag—Royal Dowry, by *Royal Charger	Tom Gentry	Kazao Nakamura	KeeJul	$1,600,000
1980	Lichine	c	Lyphard—Stylish Genie, by Bagdad	Mrs. George F. Getty et al.	BBA (England)	KeeJul	$1,700,000
1981	Ballydoyle	c	Northern Dancer—South Ocean, by New Providence	Windfields Farm	BBA (Ireland)	KeeJul	$3,500,000
1982	Empire Glory	c	Nijinsky II—Spearfish, by Fleet Nasrullah	Glencoe Farm	BBA (Ireland)	KeeJul	$4,250,000
1983	Snaafi Dancer	c	Northern Dancer—My Bupers, by Bupers	Crescent Farm	Aston Upthorpe Stud	KeeJul	$10,200,000
1985	Seattle Dancer	c	Nijinsky II—My Charmer, by Poker	Warner L. Jones Jr.	BBA (England)	KeeJul	$13,100,000

ALL-TIME TOP-SELLING WEANLING COLTS

PRICE	NAME	PEDIGREE	CONSIGNOR	BUYER	SALE	YEAR
$4,424,438	Padua's Pride	Caerleon—Doff the Derby, by Master Derby	Barronstown Stud, Ireland	BBA (England)	TatFoa	1997
$2,400,000	Unnamed	Storm Cat—Spain, by Thunder Gulch	Three Chimneys Sales, agent	Dromoland Farm	KeeNov	2003
$1,500,000	King Charlemagne	Nureyev—Race the Wild Wind, by Sunny's Halo	Ashford Stud, agent	Demi O'Byrne	KeeNov	1998
$1,450,000	Juniper	Danzig—Montage, by Alydar	Taylor Made Sales Agency, agent	Demi O'Byrne	KeeNov	1998
$1,400,000	Winthrop	Storm Cat—Tinnitus, by Restless Wind	John R. Gaines Thoroughbreds, agent	Demi O'Byrne	KeeNov	1996
$1,400,000	Restoration	Sadler's Wells—Madame Est Sortie, by Longleat	Eaton Sales, agent	M.W. Miller III, agent	KeeNov	1999
$1,300,000	New Trieste	A.P. Indy—Lovlier Linda, by Vigors	John R. Gaines Thoroughbreds, agent	Paul Shanahan	KeeNov	1999
$1,175,000	Razeen	Northern Dancer—Secret Asset, by Graustark	Hermitage	Darley Stud Management	Jones Dispersal	1987
$1,100,000	Hold That Tiger	Storm Cat—Beware of the Cat, by Caveat	Lane's End, agent	Demi O'Byrne	KeeNov	2000
$1,000,000	Swiss Desert	Danzig—Strictly Raised, by Raise a Native	Bruce Hundley	Gainsborough Farm	KeeNov	1989

ALL-TIME TOP-SELLING WEANLING FILLIES

PRICE	NAME	PEDIGREE	CONSIGNOR	BUYER	SALE	YEAR
$2,942,730	My Typhoon	Giant's Causeway—Urban Sea, by Miswaki	Irish National Stud	Live Oak Stud	TatFoa	2002
$2,500,000	Magic of Life	Seattle Slew—Larida, by Northern Dancer	The Newstead Farm Trust	BBA (England)	Newstead Disp.	1985
$2,300,000	Ghashtah	Nijinsky II—My Charmer, by Poker	Hermitage	Shadwell	Jones Disp.	1987
$1,646,106	All Too Beautiful	Sadler's Wells—Urban Sea, by Miswaki	A Partnership	Demi O'Byrne	TatFoa	2001
$1,500,000	Teeming	Storm Cat—Better Than Honour, by Deputy Minister	Hill 'n' Dale Sales Agency, agent	Josham Farms	KeeNov	2001
$1,400,000	Unnamed	Storm Cat—Serena's Tune, by Mr. Prospector	Hill 'n' Dale Sales Agency, agent	Dell Ridge Farm	KeeNov	2003
$1,400,000	Secret Thyme	Storm Cat—Garden Secrets, by Time for a Change	Eaton Sales, agent	Brushwood Stable	KeeNov	2003
$1,200,000	She's a Beauty	Storm Cat—Now That's Funny, by Saratoga Six	Gaines-Gentry Thoroughbreds	T. Hyde	KeeNov	2000
$1,200,000	Net Dancer	Nureyev—Doubles Partner, by Damascus	Bruce Hundley	E. Hudson	KeeNov	1989
$1,200,000	Tide Cat	Storm Cat—Maytide, by Naskra	John R. Gaines Thoroughbreds, agent	SOS Farms	KeeNov	1998

ALL-TIME TOP-SELLING BROODMARES

PRICE	NAME	SIRE/DAM	COVERING SIRE	CONSIGNOR	BUYER	SALE	YEAR
$7,100,000	Cash Run	Seeking the Gold—Shared Interest	Storm Cat	Taylor Made Sales Agency, agent	John Magnier	KeeNov	2003
$7,000,000	Miss Oceana	Alydar—Kittiwake	Northern Dancer	The Newstead Farm Trust	Foxfield	Newstead Disp.	1985
$7,000,000	Korveya	Riverman—Konafa	Woodman	Claiborne Farm, agent	Reynolds Bell Jr., agent	KeeNov	1998
$6,100,000	Windsharp	Lear Fan—Yes She's Sharp	Gone West	Mill Ridge Sales, agent	John Ferguson Bloodstock	KeeNov	2003
$6,000,000	Priceless Fame	Irish Castle—Comely Nell	Seattle Slew	Highclere, agent for Joseph O. Morrissey	Darley Stud Management	FTK Nov	1984
$5,500,000	Princess Rooney	Verbatim—Parrish Princess	Danzig	Stone Farm	Wichita Equine	KeeNov	1985
$5,400,000	Life's Magic	Cox's Ridge—Fire Water	Mr. Prospector	Mel Hatley Racing Stables	Eugene V. Klein	KeeNov	1986
$5,300,000	Spain	Thunder Gulch—Drina	Storm Cat	Three Chimneys Sales, agent	Dromoland Farm	KeeNov	2003
$5,250,000	Producer	Nashua—Marion	Northern Dancer	Walnut Green (Jones Bros.), agent	BBA (England)	KeeNov	1983
$5,000,000	Mackie	Summer Squall—Glowing Tribute	Mr. Prospector	Eaton Sales, agent	Britton House Stud	KeeJan	2000

ALL-TIME TOP-SELLING JUVENILES

PRICE	NAME	SEX	PEDIGREE	CONSIGNOR	BUYER	SALE	YEAR
$4,500,000	Unnamed	c	Fusaichi Pegasus—Hidden Storm, by Storm Cat	Kirkwood Stables, agt.	Fusao Sekiguchi	FTF Feb	2004
$3,100,000	Unnamed	c	Stephen Got Even—Blacktie Bid, by Black Tie Affair	Niall Brennan Stables, agt.	John Ferguson	FTF Feb	2004
$2,700,000	Diamond Fury	c	Sea of Secrets—Swift Spirit, by Tasso	Sequel Bloodstock, agt.	Charles Fipke	BarMar	2003
$2,000,000	La Salle Street	c	Not for Love—Three Grand, by Assert (Ire)	H.T. Stables, agt.	Demi O'Byrne	KeeApr	1999
$2,000,000	Morocco	c	Brocco—Roll Over Baby, by Rollin On Over	Sequel Bloodstock, agt.	The Thoroughbred Corp	BarMar	1999
$2,000,000	Gotham City	c	Saint Ballado—What a Reality, by In Reality	Jerry Bailey Sales Agency	David J. Shimmon	BarMar	2000
$2,000,000	Unnamed	f	Awesome Again—Sassy Pants, by Saratoga Six	Jerry Bailey Sales Agency	John Ferguson	BarMar	2004
$1,950,000	Yonaguska	c	Cherokee Run—Marital Spook, by Silver Ghost	Niall Brennan Stables, agt.	Demi O'Byrne	FTF Feb	2000

Success Stories

Beautiful Pleasure
bay filly, 1995
Maudlin—Beautiful Bid,
by Baldski

The notes on the catalog page denote a "big, powerful individual, racy and with a ton of presence, the best-looking horse in the sale." An additional penciled notation reads "even from a distance a grand-looking colt." Big, powerful, and grand, yes. But a colt she wasn't. Bred by Farnsworth Farm in Florida, Beautiful Pleasure was consigned to the 1997 Keeneland April sale of two-year-olds where John C. Oxley purchased the Amazon of a filly for $480,000. She spent the next five years proving the notations weren't exaggerations. She

won 10 races from 25 starts. In 1999 she won her last three races, all grade Is, including the Breeders' Cup Distaff. In addition to an Eclipse Award as champion older female for 1999, Beautiful Pleasure earned a career total of $2,734,078. In 2003 she produced her first foal, a Thunder Gulch colt.

Funny Cide
chestnut gelding, 2000
Distorted Humor—Belle's Good Cide,
by Slewacide

Hip #320 from the McMahon of Saratoga Thoroughbreds consignment to the 2001 Saratoga August preferred sale (see his catalog page in Ch. 3, page 59)

SKIP DICKSTEIN

Beautiful Pleasure.

proved a real bargain. As a yearling son of a first-year sire, he brought only $22,000; as a racehorse named Funny Cide, he won the Kentucky Derby, Preakness Stakes, and an Eclipse Award as champion three-year-old male of 2003. The first gelding since Clyde Van Dusen in 1929 and the first New-York bred to win the Derby, Funny Cide has become a fan favorite and something of a cultural phenomenon with a variety of merchandise available: shirts and hats, snowglobes, and even beer. The WinStar Farm-bred to this point has earned more than two million dollars for the Sackatoga Stables, and since he is a gelding, no outside activities will distract him from future racing. He began his four-year-old campaign with an allowance win at Gulfstream Park in Florida.

Fusaichi Pegasus
bay colt, 1997
Mr. Prospector—Angel Fever,
by Danzig

From the very beginning his story was not one of which fairy tales are made. A bay son of leading sire Mr. Prospector, Fusaichi Pegasus came to the 1998 Keeneland July sale in the Stone Farm consignment of his co-breeder Arthur B. Hancock III (with Stonerside Farm) possessing the commanding presence of a superhero (the colt's nickname at the farm was Superman) and looking like a million. But by the time the bidding had ended, it took four times that amount to take him home. Owned by Fusao Sekiguchi, the colt began his sophomore season with four straight wins.

Fusaichi Pegasus' victory in the Wood Memorial elevated him to favorite status for the Kentucky Derby, a race he duly won. He added the Jerome Handicap before retiring to stud with six wins from nine starts and $1,994,400 in earnings. He was syndicated for stud duty at Ashford Stud in Kentucky for a figure reportedly between 60 and 70 million dollars. With a price tag of four million dollars, Fusaichi Pegasus had hardly seemed such a bargain.

John Henry
bay gelding, 1975
Ole Bob Bowers—Once Double,
by Double Jay

John Henry is a Horatio Alger hero in horsehide. Robert Lehman, the breeder, consigned the small, plain yearling to the Keeneland January sale where John Callaway signed the ticket for $1,100. The following January, John Henry sold again at Keeneland, this time for $2,200, to Harold Snowden. It was the last public sale John Henry would have to face; however, it wouldn't be the last time he was sold, finally ending up in the barn of Sam Rubin for $25,000. Luck and pluck took the little gelding the rest of the way — to seven championship titles including two for Horse of the Year. He won 39 of his 83 races and earned $6,591,860, quite a rate of return for an original investment of $1,100, or even a final $25,000. He retired to the Kentucky Horse Park near Lexington. Time may have withered his athleticism, but age has not staled his curmudgeonly behavior, nor his love of doughnuts.

Seattle Slew

dark bay colt, 1974
Bold Reasoning—My Charmer,
by Poker

Newcomers to racing, Mickey and Karen Taylor, along with partners Jim and Sally Hill, plunked down $17,500 at the Fasig-Tipton summer yearling sale in 1975. In exchange they received a dark bay colt that would change their lives forever. A champion at two, Seattle Slew reeled off victory after victory at three and remained undefeated through the Triple Crown races. He was champion at three and at four and was voted Horse of the Year as a three-year-old. When he retired from racing at the end of 1978, he had earned $1,208,726 with 14 wins in 17 starts. Based on syndication figures of forty shares, the owners sold a half interest to the colt for $6,000,000, and Slew went off to stud duty at Spendthrift Farm. As a sire he was as unqualified a success as he had been as a racehorse, siring runners that have earned more than $80 million. Seattle Slew died in 2002 and is buried at Hill 'n' Dale Farm near Lexington, Kentucky.

Serena's Song.

Serena's Song

bay filly, 1992
Rahy—Imagining,
by Northfields

For a mere $150,000 Bob and Beverly Lewis hit the mother lode when they purchased a yearling bay filly from the Bridlewood consignment to the 1993 Keeneland July sale. That trip to the sales was not the filly's first. She had sold as a weanling the previous November for $42,000. It was a nice pinhook for Bridlewood, a return of 360 percent. But that figure was only a harbinger of what was to come.

By the end of her two-year-old racing season, Serena's Song had more than repaid her purchase price, winning the Landaluce, Oak Leaf, and Starlet stakes. Her sophomore season was even more impressive as she won nine of her 13 starts, including the Haskell over her male counterparts, and more than $1.5 million. As a further reward she

Seattle Slew.

won an Eclipse for best three-year-old filly. She repeated her million dollar earnings as a four-year-old with important victories in the Santa Maria and Hempstead handicaps among others.

A rarity in today's racing world, she retired with 38 starts over three seasons and earnings of $3,283,388. She proved just as valuable in her second career. Three of her offspring have sold at public auction: the stakes-winning Serena's Tune (by Mr. Prospector) for $1 million; group I-winning Sophisticat (Storm Cat) for $3.4 million; and current two-year-old Harlington (Unbridled) for $2.8 million. The $150,000 has returned more than $10.4 million. Any stock market investor would like such a rate of return.

Silverbulletday

bay filly, 1996
Silver Deputy—Rokeby Rose,
by Tom Rolfe

She was the people's choice. Why shouldn't she be? She was the genuine thing, the real deal. She attracted fans like a heatwave. In her first two years of racing, Silverbulletday hardly put a foot wrong. Having colorful connections didn't hurt her press either. Trained by Bob Baffert for Mike Pegram, the daughter of Silver Deputy won six of her seven starts at two. She was named champion two-year-old filly. As a three-year-old, she carried a string of eight straight victories into the Belmont Stakes against a field that included dual classic winner Charismatic. For the third straight year there were

BARBARA D. LIVINGSTON

Silverbulletday.

Triple Crown hopes, and the thousands of fans that gathered made her the third choice in a power-packed field. After setting the pace through the first mile, she gave way and finished seventh to eventual winner Lemon Drop Kid. No shame in that performance. Returned to her own division, she ran off three more victories including the Alabama Stakes at Saratoga. At year's end she was champion three-year-old filly, joining such greats as Go for Wand and Ruffian as juvenile filly champions to repeat at three. She won only one of five starts at four and retired with 15 wins from 23 starts and earnings of $3,093,207. Not bad for a $155,000 yearling purchase from the Fasig-Tipton Kentucky July sale. To this date, she has produced two foals: a 2002 A.P. Indy colt and a 2003 Storm Cat filly.

Skip Away.

Skip Away
Grey colt, 1993
Skip Trial—Ingot Way,
by Diplomat Way

There's just something about a grey horse that catches the eye. Especially when that grey coat is on a frame that will grow to 16.2 hands with good bone, a strong shoulder, and the hindquarters to match. That's exactly what Sonny and Carolyn Hine saw when they purchased a two-year-old colt from the Ocala Breeders' February sale for $30,000.

Skip Away might have been slow to round into form, but the potential always lay beneath the power. After breaking his maiden in his third start, he finished his juvenile year with placings in three stakes, including the Cowdin and Remsen stakes. On the road to the classics, there was a pothole or two. After winning the Blue Grass Stakes, he ran twelfth in the Kentucky Derby but rebounded for second-place finishes in the Preakness and Belmont. He finished the year in stellar fashion, winning the Haskell Invitational, the Woodbine Million, and the Jockey Club Gold Cup. He earned an Eclipse as best three-year-old colt and more than $2 million. His first year as an older horse was his best financially. He repeated his Jockey Club Gold Cup victory, and he added the Breeders' Cup Classic in the fastest time ever. He was voted champion older horse.

At five he won his first seven starts, all stakes, and repeated as champion older horse. His exemplary record through most of the year also meant Horse of the Year honors as well. Skip Away retired to stud with earnings of more than $9 million and victories in ten grade I stakes.

Sky Beauty
bay filly, 1990
Blushing Groom—Maplejinsky,
by Nijinsky II

Sky Beauty may have been a Kentucky girl, but she possessed a New York state of mind. Bred in the Bluegrass by Sugar Maple Farm, a New York-based farm, she made her debut at the epicenter of American racing, Saratoga. Consigned to the 1991 Saratoga select sale by her breeder, the yearling daughter of Blushing Groom pleased Georgia Hofmann well enough that the breeder of Sky Beauty's dam laid down $355,000 to take the daughter home. Sky Beauty repaid that trust from the outset.

She showed she loved her adopted state by winning all of her stakes races there, and there were many, including the three races that were then considered the filly triple crown: the Acorn, Mother Goose, and Coaching Club American Oaks. To this skein of victories, she added the venerated Alabama at Saratoga. Despite her success she failed to win an Eclipse Award at three but rectified that deficiency the next year when she was named champion older female. From 21 starts she won 15 races and finished out of the top three only twice. She earned $1,336,000. As residual value, two of the foals bred by Hofmann sold at public auction: a Danzig colt (Bestyoucanbe) for $500,000 and a Storm Cat filly (Storming Beauty) for $1,200,000. Sky Beauty herself returned to the sales ring after her owner died and brought $2,850,000 at the 1999 Keeneland November sale.

BARBARA D. LIVINGSTON

Sky Beauty.

91

Xtra Heat

Bay filly, 1998
Dixieland Heat—Begin,
by Hatchet Man

The third time might not have been the charm, but it was better than the second time and worse than the first, at least as far as sales ring prices were concerned. But in the end, any of them would have been good value. As a weanling, Xtra Heat sold for $9,100 at the to recompense her purchase price; the remainder of her career would be written in nothing but black ink. She strung stakes races together like pearls: five here, six there, until she had accumulated twenty-five of them, the magic number needed to break Susan's Girl's distaff record for the most stakes wins. She was also named champion three-year-old filly of 2001. Near the end of her four-year-old season, she was once again offered for sale, but there

Xtra Heat.

ANNE M. EBERHARDT

1998 Keeneland November sale. She next sold for $4,700 at Ocala Breeders' Sales' August yearling sale. As a two-year-old at the 2000 Fasig-Tipton Midlantic May sale, trainer John Salzman purchased Xtra Heat for $5,000. Racing for a partnership, Xtra Heat broke her maiden in her first start, a maiden claiming race at Laurel. Eligible to be claimed for $25,000, she won by a half-length. It was the only time she would run for a tag. The $8,550 winnings were more than enough would be no bargain basement price this time. At the Fasig-Tipton Kentucky November select sale, she failed to reach her reserve and was bid in at $1.7 million; however, Classic Star Stable purchased her privately following the sale and she won two of her last three starts for her new owner. She retired with 26 wins in 35 starts (she finished worse than third only twice) and earnings of $2,389,635. She was bred to leading sire Gone West for the 2004 foaling season.

Frequently Asked Questions

How can I get a catalog?

You can get a catalog for any sale by contacting the sales company offices and requesting one — by phone, e-mail, fax, or written request. Also, you might ask to be put on a list to receive catalogs for any upcoming auctions. Once you are on the mailing list, many sales companies send out cards so that you can check off the sales you are interested in for the year. By returning the card to the sales company office, you should receive catalogs for the indicated sales. Many sales companies have their catalogs online at their web sites, making it possible to download the information you need from the web sites.

How do I go about establishing credit?

It is a good idea for first-time buyers to establish a line of credit before attending a horse auction. Once you have received your sales catalogs, you should be able to find information about payment procedures in the first few pages of the catalog. As the procedures might vary among the different sales companies, it is best to read the pertinent information for each sales company. If there are any questions, contact that sales company directly. Most catalogs contain a buyer registration form and an application for credit. These forms are often found online and may be completed online or downloaded, printed, completed, and returned to the sales company. These should be on file in the sales company office well in advance of the sale. Since it is sometimes easy to be caught up in the moment and you have fallen for that chestnut filly that is "a real bargain" you just have to have, you might also check the sales company's policy on spur-of-the moment purchases, where credit has not been established beforehand.

How do I pay and how long do I have to pay?

If you have established a line of credit prior to the sale and have been approved, there is usually a grace period before payment is due. Check with the individual sales company to find out how much of an extension is granted. You may also pay by personal check, cash, wire transfers, cashier's check, etc. Usually these kinds of transactions must be taken care of shortly after the hammer falls. Check with the sales company to find out how long a buyer has to settle up in the office. Once again, it expedites matters to have your financial information in the sales office prior to the sale. If you have decided to go through a bloodstock agent, the agency will help you handle the payment procedure; however, you should fill out and file an authorized agent form with the sales office prior to the sale.

How can I get a reserved seat?

It is not necessary to have a seat to buy a horse; however, it certainly gives you some support if you suddenly feel faint from having spent more than you had budgeted for. Reserved seating is usually available at most sales and historically is given to buyers who have purchased with that sales company before. To get a reserved seat, you should fill out a seating request form usually found in the catalog. Preference for reserved seating is given to those who are long-time patrons or to those who have already established credit. The seating request may also be available online, so check the company's web site.

How and when can I find the horses, barns, and consignors?

Most sales catalogs contain a map of the grounds that indicates the barns and their positions relative to the sales pavilion. The catalog page for each horse indicates its barn number, consignor, and hip number. Most consignors are very helpful and have put up colorful signs at the barns to let you know where they are located. The card person for each consignment will make sure you see the horses you wish to inspect. If you have a lot of horses that you want to see, it's best to plan ahead and organize your trip through the barn area. Most often horses are available a day or two prior to the sale. This holds especially true for a one-day or two-day sale. Larger sales with more sales days vary. The select horses may be there two or three full days prior to the date of sale; after the select sale portion, horses usually ship in one day, are available for inspection late that afternoon, all the next day, and then up until they are being readied to go to the sale ring. An out list, which is available online or in the sales office, lets you know if the horse you are interested in is still in the sale, so it's good to check the outs every morning before you start your rounds.

ROB CARR

Reserved seating is a nice option if you plan to frequent a particular sale.

How can I get the sales results throughout the sale?

The sales companies provide sheets of the previous day's results. These may be picked up at the entrance or at the sales office. Also, many sales companies provide online results that are available perhaps twenty to thirty minutes after a horse has sold. If you want more immediate results, you can contact the sales office and inquire about any specific hip number. If you have just come back to your senses after signing a sales ticket and the adrenaline has stopped pumping, and you can't remember how much you just spent, you can always look up at the figures on the bid board.

Where can I get pedigree information, catalog updates, etc.?

Do your homework ahead of time. Sales companies often offer updates for horses in their sales on the company's web site. Check the web site to find out if this service is available.

Many consignors provide updates about the horses in their consignments. As you inspect the horses in the barn area, someone working for the consignor will often come around and update you on anything that has changed in the family since the catalog was written. It might be earnings updates, or additional stakes winners in the family, or recent winners in the family, but you can make note of these updates on your catalog page. As a service to the buyers, many times companies like The Jockey Club with its Equine Line will update any hip numbers in the catalog for free. You need to check with the sales companies to see if this service will be available. If not, you can order reports from these pedigree research companies.

What is the repository?

The repository is the area on the sales grounds where X-rays (radiographs) and other medical information are kept for inspection. Check with the individual sales companies to see which views are required for inclusion in the repository and how long before the sale the images must be taken. Usually included are various views of knees, hocks, fetlocks, and stifles.

Who has the ability to look at radiographs and files in the repository?

Generally speaking this task should be left to a veterinarian who is trained in reading and interpreting the information in the repository. Check with the individual sales companies to see if there is any limitation on who can make use of the repository. Certain consignors may ask that the information be limited to veterinarians only.

What are the available hours for viewing material in the repository?

You need to check with the individual sales companies to find out the dates that the repository is open for each sale and the daily hours the material is available for scrutiny.

Should I hire a veterinarian?

A veterinarian, more specifically a large animal veterinarian who specializes in equine care, has been trained to interpret medical information for horses and is far more adept at doing so than most lay people, especially someone who is new to buying horses. So, if you want to get the most professional advice possible, it might be in your best interest to hire a veterinarian.

Scoping is an important pre-sale test.

What is an endoscopic examination?

The endoscopic examination (commonly called "scoping") evaluates the upper airway of the horse by passing a flexible fiber optic tube called an endoscope through the horse's nostril. Veterinarians then can examine the size of the horse's airway and any disorders that might affect the horse's ability to race.

What is a cribber?

The term "cribber" is used to denote a horse that places its front teeth on a hard surface, usually the top of a fence or a stall door, and sucks in air. Cribbing is believed to be an acquired habit and an addictive behavior. If a horse is a cribber, it must be announced before the horse is sold.

What is a cryptorchid?

A cryptorchid is a male horse that has either one testicle or both testicles undescended into the scrotum. Most horses with this condition have only one undescended testicle. The horse may also be referred to as a ridgling. There have been many ridglings that have gone on to race and be successful sires.

Ridglings are announced pre-bidding.

What is a wobbler?

A horse that is a wobbler has a condition caused by compression on the spinal cord. It is marked by a lack of coordination. The condition might be a result of poor nutrition, injury, or rapid growth. A wobbler usually is returnable if the buyer follows the procedures set forth in the catalog.

Are there any warranties of sale?

Warranties of sale are described in the conditions of sale, which are usually found in the first few pages of the catalog. As a prospective buyer, it is your responsibility to familiarize yourself with the conditions of sale and to find out what things are and aren't warranted. If you have any questions, be sure to contact the sales company office and have someone go over any specific questions you might have. Warranties may vary from type of sale to type of sale and from sales company to sales company. Warranties might also have a specific time limit, so it might be best to have your new horse examined by a veterinarian before it leaves the sales grounds. Generally speaking, except for the limited warranties discussed in the conditions of sale, all sales are "as is."

How can I find out if a horse is Breeders' Cup nominated or state-bred nominated?

These are usually stated on the catalog page corresponding with the horse's hip number, usually in the bottom left-hand margin. You might see printed "Registered New York-bred" or "Registered Florida-bred." Black type might declare that the horse is "Breeders' Cup nominated." To double-check, you might also ask the horse's consignor, who should be aware of these kinds of nominations. In addition, always check with the sales office as errors can occur.

When do I get The Jockey Club registration certificate?

Upon settlement of payment the sales company office issues a stable release so that the horse can be

Double-check the hip number to be sure you are bidding on the correct horse.

removed from the sales grounds. Later the sales company sends The Jockey Club registration certificate, in other words "when the check clears."

What do I do if I bought the wrong horse?

Before you begin bidding, look at the bid board to make sure the number corresponds to the horse you want to buy. If you do think you bought the wrong horse, immediately notify sales officials. Some auction companies videotape the proceedings in defense of such claims. However, a sales company sometimes will send a mistakenly purchased horse through the ring again if time and circumstances permit. But all buyers should know that when the gavel falls and the auctioneer says the magic word "Sold," ownership of the horse has passed from the seller to the buyer.

How do you go about rescinding a sale if warranted?

A written notice to the sales company in a timely manner as stipulated in the catalog starts the process.

When do I go about taking actual possession?

Ownership has passed to you at the fall of the hammer; however, most consignors will be glad to feed and water your horse until you can have it removed from the sales grounds, if that is within a reasonable amount of time. The responsibility has passed to you, and you have to make sure that your new purchase is well cared for.

How do I make vanning/shipping arrangements?

As a serious buyer, you should have already made arrangements for a farm to board new purchases and a van company to transport them. You will be given a stable release to give to the van company so that your new horses may be removed from the grounds. Van companies usually have booths around the sales pavilion, so making arrangements to have the horse moved is not difficult.

If I buy a mare at public auction who is in foal and she does not deliver a live foal, do I get a refund on the stud fee?

The buyer is not entitled to a refund. The stallion season contract is between the original owner (seller) of the mare and the stallion owner. Most live foal stallion season contracts convert to a no guarantee season when the mare is catalogued for auction. You should try and get a copy of a season contract.

Glossary

Agent — a person who has the authority to conduct business for another: for example, to buy or sell horses.

Arbitration — a legal hearing of a dispute between two parties by an impartial third party agreed upon by the contending parties.

Auctioneer — a person conducting the public sale of property that will belong to the highest bidder.

Authorized agent form — a notarized document that empowers one person to act on behalf of another during the sale. The document should be on file in the sales office prior to the start of the sale.

Barren — a term used to describe a mare that was bred during a breeding season but did not conceive.

Bay — a classification of color that runs the gamut of light tan to dark brown and marked by a black mane and tail and by black points on the legs with the exception of any white that might be there.

Bid board — the sign that displays the selling horse's hip number and also follows the monetary progression of the bidding.

Bid spotter — an employee of the auction company. Bid spotters are scattered around the sales venue and as each horse is auc-

tioned, act as an intermediary by conveying a bidder's acceptance of the amount asked back to the auctioneer.

Bidder — a person who seeks to purchase a horse by indicating acceptance of an amount the auctioneer is asking. A bidder may be bidding against other bidders or against a reserve bid.

Black type — a sales catalog designation for stakes winners and stakes-placed horses. Stakes winners are designated by bold-faced capital letters while stakes-placed horses are bold-faced. Not all stakes races are eligible for black-type designation.

Bloodstock agent — a person who specializes in buying and selling horses, breeding seasons, and stallion shares. A bloodstock agent may be enlisted to represent and advise both buyers and sellers.

Book — a designation of one of a number of catalogs for the same sale. Sales with a large number of horses must divide their catalogs into more than one volume. Each volume is designated as a book; e.g. Book 1 may cover hips 1-700; Book 2, hips 701-1440.

Bottom line — a term used to refer to a horse's female family.

Broodmare — a mare that has been bred and is used for breeding purposes.

Broodmare prospect — a filly or mare that has not been bred but is capable of being used for breeding purposes.

Broodmare sire — the father of the mare in a pedigree line.

Buy-back — a horse offered at public auction that did not make its reserve bid and was, therefore, not sold.

Buyer registration form — a document filed with the sales company before the sale allowing credit verification and requesting approval to buy.

By — a word used to designate the sire of a particular horse; e.g. Hip #3 is a bay colt *by* Seattle Slew.

Catalog page — the buyer's source of information about each hip number in the sale. A typical catalog page lists the consignor, the hip number, the location of the horse on the sales grounds, the pedigree, sire statistics, maternal bloodlines, etc.

Chestnut — a classification of color that ranges in shades of gold, red, and near brown. A chestnut horse will not have a black mane, tail, or points on its legs.

Colt — an ungelded (entire) male horse four years old and younger.

Commission — the fee charged by an agent or sales company for negotiating a transaction. Usually, a commission is a percentage of the sales price.

Conditions of sale — the legal terms that govern how an auction is conducted. These include such things as acceptable methods of payment, warranties and their limitations, resolution of disputes, etc. The conditions of sale will usually be found in the catalog. The conditions of sale might also be announced by the auctioneer prior to each sale session.

Conformation — the way a horse is put together physically.

Consignor — the person or agency responsible for offering a horse for sale at auction.

Credit request — a document submitted to the sales company prior to the sale that authorizes the sales company to investigate credit.

Cribber — a horse that habitually latches onto an object with its teeth and swallows or sucks air.

Dam — a horse's mother.

Dark bay or brown — a classification of color that ranges from a deep brown to a dark brown, resembling black. Brown hair will be found on the muzzle, flank, inner forearms, or thighs.

Drop of the hammer — the act of the auctioneer pounding his gavel and indicating the final bid. The drop of the hammer is usually accompanied by the auctioneer announcing, "Sold."

Female family — in a pedigree the mother's line, from female generation to female generation all the way back to the original ancestress.

Filly — a female horse four years old and under that has never been bred.

Foal — a baby horse that has not yet been weaned from its mother.

Full brother — a male horse that has the same sire and dam as other horses. The famous sires Bull Dog and Sir Gallahad III were full brothers, both being by Teddy out of Plucky Liege.

Full sister — a female horse that has the same sire and dam as other horses.

Gavel — the hammer used by the auctioneer to punctuate the auctioning process.

Gelding — a male horse that has had his testicles removed. Armed, Forego, and Kelso were famous geldings.

Graded race — a classification of select races in North America and patterned after the European group races. These races are categorized as grade I, grade II, and grade III. For example, the Kentucky Derby is a grade I event.

Grey/roan — a classification of color recognized by The Jockey Club. Grey horses have a mixture of white hair with their base color (could be born as bays, chestnuts, etc.) Grey horses become more and more white as they age. Roan horses also have a mix of white hair with a base color, but they stay the same color throughout their life.

Group race — a classification of select races in Europe and other parts of the world like Australia, etc. These races are categorized as group I, group II, and group III. For example, the Epsom Derby, Prix de l'Arc de Triomphe, and Melbourne Cup are group I events.

Half brother — a male horse that has the same dam as other horses but a different sire. For example, Belmont winner A.P. Indy and Preakness winner Summer Squall are half brothers, both being out of Weekend Surprise, but A.P. Indy is by Seattle Slew and Summer Squall is by Storm Bird.

Half sister — a female horse that has the same dam as other horses but a different sire.

Hand — the unit of measurement for a horse's height. Each hand is the equivalent of four inches. No horse would be 15.4 hands; rather it would be 16 hands. A horse's height is measured from the ground to the withers.

Hip number — how horses are referred to during a sale. The term derives from the fact that a sticker with a number on it is placed on each horse's hip as a means of identifying that horse. The number corresponds to the corresponding lot number in the catalog. For example, Hip #1 will be the first horse in the catalog and the first horse to be sold in the ring.

Holding area — the part of the sales pavilion where the horses are kept before entering the auction ring. This area often gives prospective buyers a last chance to inspect a horse.

Horse — any ungelded male five years old and older.

Horse of racing age — any Thoroughbred two years old and older that is eligible to compete in racing.

In foal — a mare is said to be "in foal" when she is pregnant.

Inbred — having one or more common ancestors within the first five generations. In a five-cross pedigree if the name Northern Dancer appears in the third generation on the sire's side of the pedigree and in the fourth generation on the dam's side, the horse is said to be inbred 3x4 to Northern Dancer.

Inspection — prior to a sale, prospective buyers have the opportunity to go to the consignor's barn on the sales ground and look over any horses that have piqued their interest. The catalog should specify the times and the dates for inspection.

Listed race — those stakes races just below graded and group races in quality. These races are designated by [L] on the catalog page.

Mare — a female horse five years old and older or a younger female horse that has been bred.

Out — a horse that has been withdrawn from the sale. The list of outs can be found on the web site prior to the sale, or a list of the day's outs can be picked up at the sales office. So, before you make the pilgrimage all the way to Barn 48 to inspect Hip #1033 on that cold, windy, wet day, check the list of outs to see if the horse is still in.

Out of — a term used to designate the dam of a particular horse. For example, Secretariat was a chestnut colt by Bold Ruler *out of* Somethingroyal.

Outcross — having no common ancestors within the first five generations. Of the 62 horses in a five-cross pedigree, there will be no duplicated names.

Pavilion — the building where the sale is held.

Pedigree — the family tree, listing all the horse's ancestors by generation. Most catalog pages have a three-cross pedigree.

Pinhook — buying a horse in hopes of selling it later at a higher price. For example, many weanlings are purchased to be resold as yearlings.

Produce record — the listing of the offspring of a mare. The catalog pages for breeding stock sales will have a produce record for the mares being sold.

Registration certificate — the document that acts as the "title" to the horse. Originally issued by The Jockey Club, it passes from owner to owner with the sale of the horse.

Repository — the area on the sales grounds where X-rays and other medical information are kept for inspection.

Reserve — the minimum price set by the seller for a horse at auction.

RNA — the letters used in the results sheet to indicate that a horse did not reach its reserve price (Reserve Not Attained).

Restricted race — a stakes race below the graded, group level that has certain stipulations involved. For example, the stakes may be limited to Florida-bred horses only. These races are designated in the sales catalogs by an [R].

Ridgling — a male horse that has one or both testes undescended; also called a cryptorchid.

Sales catalog — the guide to the horses being sold. All that's missing is a photo. A page is devoted to each horse entered in the sale and gives pertinent information concerning pedigree, race record, etc. The catalog also includes the conditions of sale. It may also include a guide to local restaurants and hotels.

Scoping — a procedure in which a veterinarian uses an endoscope to examine the upper airway in a horse.

Seating request form — a document submitted to the sales company to apply for seats in the sales arena.

Select sale — a sale that is limited to horses chosen on pedigree and conformation.

Sire — a horse's father.

Sire blurb — the part of the catalog page that lists the sire's statistics and achievements.

Sire line — in a pedigree the line of stallions from generation to generation. For example, Secretariat is by Bold Ruler, who is by Nasrullah, who is by Nearco, etc. Sire lines trace back to one of three original stallions: Eclipse, Herod, or Matchem.

Slipped — a term used to describe a mare that aborted her foal.

Sound — a term used to describe a horse that is free from injury.

Stable release — the document that is necessary to give to security in order to remove a horse from the sales grounds.

Stakes race — a race for which an owner must pay a fee or a series of fees in order to run. Many stakes are the feature races on a track's racecard. Graded and group races are the highest echelon of stakes races.

Stakes-placed — a term that refers to a horse that finishes second or third in a stakes race.

Stallion — a male horse used for breeding.

Stallion season — a term used to describe the right to mate a mare to a stallion during one breeding year.

Stallion share — a term used to describe a proprietary interest in a stallion, giving the owner the right to breed a mare to a stallion every breeding season for as long as the share is owned or to sell that right to another. Sometimes owning a share in a stallion will result in a bonus season during a breeding year, which allows the owner to breed a second mare to that stallion.

The Jockey Club — the governing body for Thoroughbred breeding and racing.

Ticket — the document that acts as an acknowledgment of purchase. It contains the horse's hip number and the selling price. The ticket acts as a binding contract that the buyer will purchase that hip number at that price, so don't sign the ticket without checking the hip number and the price or else that lovely gray filly you thought you bought for a song may turn out to be a not-so-lovely bay that cost your entire budget.

Two-year-old in training — a kind of sale for juvenile horses that are in the early stages of being readied for racing.

Upset price — the minimum price needed to open the bidding on a horse offered at auction.

Warranty — a legal term referring to the representation that the goods will perform as promised. The conditions of sale found in the catalog outline the warranties of the sale and their limitations.

Weanling — a foal that is no longer dependent upon its dam.

X-ray — radiographs on file in the repository. Veterinarians read these radiographs in order to advise clients on purchases.

Yearling — a horse that has reached its first birthdate. Thoroughbreds become a year older on January 1, the universal birthdate for all Thoroughbreds.

Resource Guide

This listing includes the types of sales offered, the month the sale is generally held, and the location. To find out specific sales dates, contact the sales company for a complete schedule and to receive catalogs.

American Equine Sales
4061 E. Castro Valley Blvd.
Suite 276
Castro Valley, CA 94552
(510) 293-9330
www.americanequinesales.com
Two-year-olds in training
June — Alameda County Fairgrounds, Pleasanton, Calif.
Yearlings
August — Alameda County Fairgrounds

Arizona Thoroughbred Breeders Association
P.O. Box 41774, Phoenix, AZ 85050
(602) 942-1310
www.atba.net
Mixed
October — Westworld, Scottsdale, Ariz.

Arkansas Breeders' Sales Company
P.O. Box 1665, Hot Springs, AR 71902
(501) 624-6336

Arkansas Thoroughbred Sales Co.
P.O. Box 180159
Fort Smith, AR 72918
(501) 648-3402
Mixed
February, October — Barton Coliseum, State Fairgrounds, Little Rock, Ark.

Barretts Equine Ltd.
P.O. Box 2010, Pomona, CA 91769
(909) 629-3099
www.barretts.com
(For sales dates, see Ch. 2, Major Sales Companies.)

Breeders Sales Company of Louisiana
P.O. Box 24650
New Orleans, LA 70184
(504) 947-4676
www.louisianabred.com
Yearlings, mixed
September — Louisiana Downs, Bossier City, La.

California Thoroughbred Breeders Association (CTBA)
P.O. Box 60018
Arcadia, CA 91066
(626) 445-7800
www.ctba.com
Yearlings
August — Del Mar Horse Park, Del Mar, Calif.

Fair Grounds Sales Company
1751 Gentilly Blvd.
New Orleans, LA 70152
(504) 944-5515
www.fgno.com
Two-year-olds in training
March — Fair Grounds Race Course

Fasig-Tipton Company
2400 Newtown Pike
P.O. Box 13610
Lexington, KY 40583
(859) 255-1555
www.fasigtipton.com
(For all Fasig-Tipton sales dates, see Ch. 2, Major Sales Companies.)

Fasig-Tipton Florida
21001 N.W. 27th Ave.
Miami, FL 33056
(305) 626-3947

Fasig-Tipton Midlantic
356 Fair Hill Drive, Suite C
Elkton, MD 21921
(410) 392-5555

Fasig-Tipton New York
40 Elmont Road
Elmont, NY 11003
(516) 328-1800

Fasig-Tipton Texas
1000 Lone Star Parkway
Grand Prairie, TX 75050
(972) 262-0000

Finger Lakes Thoroughbred Sales
P.O. Box 301, Shortsville, NY 14548
(716) 289-8524
www.nybreds.com/GVBA/flsale.html
Mixed
*September — Finger Lakes Race
Track, Farmington, N.Y.*

Heritage Place
2829 S. MacArthur Blvd.
Oklahoma City, OK 73128
(405) 682-4551
www.heritageplace.com
Mixed
January, June, October

**Illinois Thoroughbred Breeders
and Owners Foundation**
P.O. Box 336
Caseyville, IL 62232
(618) 344-3427
www.illinoisracingnews.com
*Two-year-olds in training,
horses of racing age*
*June — Arlington Park,
Arlington Heights, Ill.*
Mixed
*Sept./Oct. — Hawthorne
Racecourse, Cicero, Ill.*

**Indiana Thoroughbred Owners
and Breeders Association**
P.O. Box 3753, Carmel, IN 46082
(800) 450-9895
www.itoba.com
Mixed
*August — Hoosier Park,
Anderson, Ind.*

**Iowa Breeders and Owners
Association**
1 Prairie Meadows Drive
Altoona, IA 50009
(515) 967-1298
www.iowathoroughbred.com
Mixed
*September — Iowa State
Fairgrounds*

Keeneland Association
4201 Versailles Road, P.O. Box 1690
Lexington, KY 40588
(859) 254-3412
www.keeneland.com
*(For sales dates, see Ch. 2,
Major Sales Companies.)*

**Louisiana Thoroughbred
Breeders Sales Co.**
P.O. Box 789, Carencro, LA 70520
(337) 896-6152
E-mail: ltbsc1@aol.com
Mixed
*April — Blackham Coliseum,
Lafayette, La.*
Mixed
August — Blackham Coliseum
Mixed
*October/November — Delta
Downs Racetrack, Vinton, La.*

Ocala Breeders' Sales Company
P.O. Box 99
1701 S.W. 60th Ave.
Ocala, FL 34478
(352) 237-2154
www.obssales.com
*(For sales dates, see Ch. 2,
Major Sales Companies.)*

Ohio Thoroughbred Breeders and Owners
6024 Harrison Ave., Suite 13
Cincinnati, OH 45248
(513) 574-5888

Oregon Thoroughbred Breeders Association
P.O. Box 17248, Portland, OR 97217
(503) 285-0658
thoroughbredinfo.com/showcase/otba.htm
Mixed
September — Oakhurst Ranch, Newburg, Ore.

Ruidoso Select Sales Company
P.O. Box 909
Ruidoso Downs, NM 88346
(505) 378-4474
www.zianet.com/rdracing/HorseSale.htm
Yearling
August — Ruidoso Downs Racetrack, Ruidoso Downs, N.M.

Thomas Sales Company
10410 N. Yale Ave., Sperry, OK 74073
(918) 288-7308
E-mail: thomas.sales@worldnet.att.net
Mixed
February, May, August, November — Expo Fairgrounds, Tulsa, Okla.

Thoroughbred Horsemen's Association of Texas
Rte. 5, Box 172, Bryan, TX 77803
(409) 823-1911

Washington Thoroughbred Breeders Association
P.O. Box 1499
Auburn, WA 98071
(253) 288-7878
www.washingtonthoroughbred.com
Yearlings
September — Emerald Downs Race Track, Auburn, Wash.
Mixed
December — Emerald Downs

Canadian Equine Sales Companies

Canadian Thoroughbred Horse Society (Ontario Division)
P.O. Box 172,
Rexdale, Ontario M9W 5L1
(416) 675-3602
www.cthsont.com
Two-year-olds in training
May — Woodbine Sales Pavilion, Rexdale, Ontario
Mixed
Dec. — Woodbine Sales Pavilion

Canadian Thoroughbred Horse Society (British Columbia Division)
17687 56-A Ave.
Surrey, British Columbia V3S 1G4
(604) 574-0145
www.cthsbc.org
Mixed
September — British Columbia

Canadian Thoroughbred Horse Society (Alberta Division)
401, 255-17 Ave., SW
Calgary, Alberta T2S 2T8
(403) 229-3609
www.cthsalta.com
Mixed
October — Alberta

Fasig-Tipton at Woodbine
Woodbine Sales Pavilion
555 Rexdale Blvd.
Rexdale, Ontario M9W 5L2
Yearling — September

Foreign Equine Sales Companies

Agence Française de Vente du Pur-Sang
32, avenue Hocquart-de-Turtot
14803 Deauville, France
+33 2 31 81 81 00
www.deauville-sales.com

Doncaster Bloodstock Sales Ltd.
Auction Mart Offices, Hawick
Roxburghshire, England TD9 9NN
+44 (0)1450 372222
www.dbsautions.com

Goffs Bloodstock Sales Ltd.
Kildare Paddocks, Kill
Co. Kildare, Ireland
+353-45-886600
www.goffs.com

William Inglis & Son Ltd.
Newmarket Stables, Sydney
Young Street, Randwick NSW,
Australia 2031
+61 (02) 9399 7999
www.inglis.com.au

Magic Millions Sales Pty Limited
28 Ascot Court, Bundall
P.O. Box 5246
Gold Coast Mail Centre
Queensland, Australia 4217
+61 (07) 5538 8933
www.magicmillions.com.au

New Zealand Bloodstock Ltd.
Karaka Sales Centre
Hingaia Road, Papakura
P.O. Box 97-447
South Auckland Mail Centre
Auckland, New Zealand
+64 9 298 0055
www.nzb.co.nz

Tattersalls Ltd.
Terrace House
Newmarket, Suffolk, England
CB8 9BT
+44 1638 665931
www.tattersalls.com

National Thoroughbred Associations

The Jockey Club
821 Corporate Drive
Lexington, KY 40503-2794
(859) 224-2700
E-mail:
comments@jockeyclub.com
www.home.jockeyclub.com

Thoroughbred Owners and Breeders Association
P.O. Box 4367
Lexington, KY 40544-4367
(859) 276-2291
E-mail: info@toba.org
www.TOBA.org

American Association of Equine Practitioners
4075 Iron Works Parkway
Lexington, KY 40511
(859) 233-0147
E-mail: aaepoffice@aaep.org
www.aaep.org

State Associations

Arizona Thoroughbred Breeders Association
P.O. Box 41774,
Phoenix, AZ 85080
(602) 942-1310
E-mail: atba@worldnet.att.net
www.atba.net

Arkansas Thoroughbred Breeders Horsemen's Association
P.O. Box 21641
Hot Springs, AR 71903-1641
Phone (501) 624-6328
E-mail: deana@atbha.com
www.atbha.com

California Thoroughbred Breeders Association
201 Colorado Place, Arcadia, CA 91007
(800) 573-2822 or (626) 445-7800
E-mail: info@ctba.com
www.ctba.com

Florida Thoroughbred Breeders' and Owners' Association
801 SW 60th Ave.
Ocala, FL 34474-1827
(352) 629-2160
E-mail: FTBOA@aol.com
www.ftboa.com

Georgia Thoroughbred Owners & Breeders Association
P.O. Box 987
Tyrone, GA 30290
(770) 451-0409
E-mail: gtoba@msn.com
www.gtoba.com

Illinois Thoroughbred Breeders & Owners Foundation
P.O. Box 336
Caseyville, IL 62232-0336
(618) 344-3427
E-mail: itboffp@apci.net
www.illinoisracingnews.com

Indiana Thoroughbred Owners & Breeders Association
P.O. Box 3753
Carmel, IN 46082-3753
(800) 450-9895
E-mail: itoba@itoba.com
www.itoba.com

Iowa Thoroughbred Breeders & Owners
1 Prairie Meadows Drive
Altoona, IA 50009
(800) 577-1097 or (515) 967-1298
E-mail:
itboa@prairiemeadows.com
www.iowathoroughbred.com

Kansas Thoroughbred Association
215 Monroe Street
Fredonia, KS 66736-1262
(620) 378-4772
E-mail: gejo@twinmounds.com

Kentucky Thoroughbred Owners and Breeders Inc.
4079 Iron Works Parkway
Lexington, KY 40511-8483
(859) 259-1643
E-mail: contact@kta-ktob.com
www.kta-ktob.com

Louisiana Thoroughbred Breeders Association
P.O. Box 24650
New Orleans, LA 70184
(800) 772-1195
or (504) 943-2149
E-mail: ltba@iamerica.net
www.louisianabred.com

Maryland Horse Breeders Association
P.O. Box 427
Timonium, MD 21094-0427
(410) 252-2100
E-mail:
info@marylandthoroughbred.com
www.marylandthoroughbred.com

Michigan Thoroughbred Owners & Breeders Association
4800 Harvey Street
Muskegon, MI 49444
(231) 798-7721
E-mail: mtoba@iserv.net
www.mtoba.com

Minnesota Thoroughbred Association
1100 Canterbury Road
Shakopee, MN 55379
(952) 496-3770
E-mail: mtassoc@voyager.net
www.mtassoc.com

**Mississippi Thoroughbred
Owners & Breeders Association**
107 Sundown
Madison, MS 39110
(601) 856-8293

**Missouri Horse Racing
Association**
19900 South State Rt. 7
Pleasant Hill, MO 64080
(816) 987-3205
E-mail: nancystorer@yahoo.com

**Nebraska Thoroughbred
Breeders Association Inc.**
P.O. Box 2215
Grand Island, NE 68802
(308) 384-4683
E-mail: ntbai@kdsi.net

**Thoroughbred Breeders'
Association of New Jersey**
444 N. Ocean Blvd., Second Floor
Ursula Plaza
Long Branch, NJ 07740
(732) 870-9718
E-mail: info@njbreds.com
www.njbreds.com

**New Mexico Horse
Breeders' Association**
P.O. Box 36869
Albuquerque, NM 87176-6869
(505) 262-0224
E-mail: nmhba@worldnet.att.net
www.nmhorsebreeders.com

**New York Thoroughbred
Breeding & Development Fund**
One Penn Plaza, Suite 725
New York, NY 10119
(212) 465-0660
E-mail: nybreds@nybreds.com
www.nybreds.com

**New York Thoroughbred
Horsemen's Association**
P.O. Box 170070,
Jamaica, NY 11417
(718) 848-5045
E-mail: nytha@aol.com
www.nytha.com

**North Carolina
Thoroughbred Breeders
Association**
2103 Orange Factory Road
Bahama, NC 27503
(919) 471-0131

**Ohio Thoroughbred
Breeders & Owners
Association**
6024 Harrison Ave.,
Suite 13
Cincinnati, OH 45248
(513) 574-5888
E-mail: gb.otbo@fuse.net

**Oklahoma Thoroughbred
Association**
2000 S.E. 15th St.,
Bldg. 450, Ste. A
Edmond, OK 73013
(405) 330-1006
E-mail: otawins@aol.com
www.otawins.com

**Oregon Thoroughbred
Breeders Association**
P.O. Box 17248
Portland, OR 97217-0248
E-mail: otba@mindspring.com
www.thoroughbredinfo.com/
    showcase/otba.htm

**Pennsylvania Horse
Breeders Association**
701 East Baltimore Pike,
Ste. C-1
Kennett Square, PA 19348
(610) 444-1050
E-mail: execsec@pabred.com
www.pabred.com

Tennessee Thoroughbred Owners and Breeders Association
P.O. Box 158504
Nashville, TN 37215
(615) 254-3376

Texas Thoroughbred Association
P.O. Box 14967, Austin, TX 78761
(512) 458-6133
E-mail:
info@texasthoroughbred.com
www.texasthoroughbred.com

Virginia Thoroughbred Association
38 Garrett St.
Warrenton, VA 20186
(540) 347-4313
E-mail: vta@vabred.org
www.vabred.org

Washington Thoroughbred Breeders Association
P.O. Box 1499
Auburn, WA 98071-1499
E-mail: maindesk@washington-thoroughbred.com
www.washingtonthoroughbred.com

West Virginia Thoroughbred Breeders Association
P.O. Box 626
Charles Town, WV 25414
(304) 728-6868

Magazines and Supplements

The Blood-Horse magazine
  The Blood-Horse *Source*
  The Blood-Horse *Auction Edge*
  The Blood-Horse *MarketWatch*
  The Blood-Horse *Stallion Register*
  The Blood-Horse *Auctions of 2003*
  The Blood-Horse *Nicks for 2004*
  The Blood-Horse *Sires of 2003*
  The Blood-Horse *Dams of 2003*

Books

Campbell, W. Cothran.
  *Lightning in a Jar:
  Catching Racing Fever.*
  Lexington, Ky.: Eclipse Press,
  2000.

Hunter, Avalyn.
  American Classic Pedigrees.
  Lexington, Ky.: Eclipse Press, 2003.

Kirkpatrick, Arnold.
  *Investing in Thoroughbreds:
  Strategies for Success.* Lexington, Ky.:
  Eclipse Press, 2001.

Loving, Nancy, DVM.
  Conformation and Performance.
  Ossining, N.Y.: Breakthrough
  Publishers, 1997.

McLean, Ken.
  Quest for the Classic Winner.
  Neenah, Wisc.: Russell Meerdink
  Co., 2000.

Metzel, Howard.
  *Own a Racehorse Without Spending
  a Fortune.* Lexington, Ky.:
  Eclipse Press, 2003.

Oliver, Robert and Bob Langrish.
  *A Photographic Guide to
  Conformation.* North Pomfret, Vt.:
  Trafalgar Square, 2003.

Proctor, Laura, ed.
  *New Thoroughbred Owners
  Handbook.* Lexington, Ky.:
  TOBA/Eclipse Press, 2003.

Toby, Milton C. and Karen L.
Perch, Ph.D.
  *Understanding Equine Business
  Basics.* Lexington, Ky.:
  Eclipse Press, 2001.

Toby, Milton C. and Karen L.
Perch, Ph.D.
Understanding Equine Law.
Lexington, Ky.: Eclipse Press, 1999.

Videos

Insider's Guide To Buying Thoroughbreds at Auction.
The Blood-Horse, 1999.

Experts Guide To Buying Weanlings.
The Blood-Horse, 2000.

Conformation: How To Buy a Winner.
The Blood-Horse, 1998.

Online Resources

The Blood-Horse
www.bloodhorse.com

Daily Racing Form
www.drf.com

Bloodstock Research Information System
www.brisnet.com

Thoroughbred Daily News
www.thoroughbreddailynews.com

The Jockey Club Information Systems
www.tjcis.com

The Jockey Club Equine Line
www.equineline.com

Thoroughbred Pedigree Query
www.pedigreequery.com

The Greatest Game
www.thegreatestgame.com

National Thoroughbred Racing Association
www.ntra.com

Thoroughbred Owners and Breeders Association
www.toba.org